A GOD THAT COULD BE REAL

A
GOD
THAT
COULD
BE REAL

SPIRITUALITY, SCIENCE, AND
THE FUTURE OF OUR PLANET

NANCY ELLEN ABRAMS

BEACON PRESS
Boston

BEACON PRESS
Boston, Massachusetts
www.beacon.org

Beacon Press books
are published under the auspices of
the Unitarian Universalist Association of Congregations.

18 17 16 15   8 7 6 5 4 3 2 1

This book is printed on acid-free paper that meets the uncoated paper
ANSI/NISO specifications for permanence as revised in 1992.

Text design and composition by Kim Arney

All drawings were done by Nicolle Rager Fuller, except for
The Uroboros of Human Identity, drawn by Nina McCurdy.

Library of Congress Cataloging-in-Publication Data
Abrams, Nancy Ellen.
A God that could be real : spirituality, science, and the
future of our planet / Nancy Ellen Abrams.
pages cm
ISBN 978-0-8070-7339-1 (hardcover : alk. paper)
ISBN 978-0-8070-7340-7 (ebook)
1. Religion and science. 2. God. I. Title.
BL240.3.A27 2015
215—dc23
2014036506

For Joel,
who expands my universe

CONTENTS

FOREWORD BY
ARCHBISHOP DESMOND TUTU

I must begin by acknowledging that I do not agree with everything that Nancy Abrams says about a scientific understanding of God. I dare say many religious believers will be deeply challenged by this book, but they will come away better for having read it, as we all do when our most cherished views are explored more deeply. Abrams presents a fascinating tour of the universe and interrogates our understanding of God with the skill of a gifted lawyer and historian of science. One is exhilarated to see that there are human beings who are as smart as she clearly is, and I am grateful that she shares her lifelong study so generously and honestly with us.

For centuries we have been stuck in a futile battle between believers and atheists, with each lampooning and denouncing each other's beliefs. It is my hope that Abrams's book can be part of a new revival of true cultural dialogue, debate, and exploration. We must move beyond the polemics and polarization that have come to characterize so much scientific-religious and interfaith discourse in our time.

The God that I worship is not one that sits in Heaven apprehensively worrying that humanity will discover his (or her) secrets. No, not at all. The God that I believe in commands us to love God with all our mind and wants us to keep learning and discovering and exploring every inch or millimeter (or nanometer) of creation. Over time, we graduate from more simplistic understandings of God to richer and more complex ones.

Far too often God is a "God of the gaps"—where we fill our lack of knowledge with a belief that there must be a God. For many centuries, when our understanding of the universe extended just to the planets and heavenly stars, we thought God resided just beyond. Then, as our knowledge of the universe expanded, we have pushed God farther and farther out in space and time. God must be much more than just a placeholder for what we do not yet know.

This book will help you clarify your own personal understanding of God. Whether you believe in the biblical interpretation of God, as I do, or in the view that Nancy presents here, or in any other view of God, you will find that your beliefs are enriched by reading Abrams's book. I am thrilled that we have the creativity and originality that is exhibited in this book, and I recommend it highly to all, religious or secular, believer or atheist, who are ready to explore honestly their understanding of the divine in our beautiful, expanding universe.

∞

DESMOND TUTU was an archbishop of the Anglican Church in South Africa until he retired in 1996. He won the Nobel Peace Prize in 1984 and the US Presidential Medal of Freedom in 2009. President Nelson Mandela chose him to chair South Africa's Truth and Reconciliation Commission, which brought to light the atrocities of apartheid, achieved racial reconciliation, and avoided civil war. He continues to be one of the world's moral leaders and an activist for social and human rights.

FOREWORD
BY PAUL DAVIES

Over the past two decades a largely sterile dispute has raged between two diametrically opposing camps: atheists and religious fundamentalists. It is surely time to move on and elevate the discussion to a higher intellectual level. This ambitious and thought-provoking book by Nancy Abrams on the interface of science and religion is a timely and welcome contribution to a more productive discussion of the topic.

The problem that many scientists have with religion is well illustrated by a debate in which I took part many years ago in London at the Royal Society, Britain's scientific academy. The panelists included the atheists Herman Bondi and Richard Dawkins. Bondi observed that some people proclaim God is nature. "I have nothing against nature," he said. Others assert that God is love. "I have nothing against love." What really upset Bondi was the absolute certainty that many religious believers profess to have in a sort of "private hot-line" to an all-knowing, all-powerful being.

Religion occupies a curious place in the world. For millions of people, following religious practice or belonging to a religious organization frames their lives in important ways and shapes, or even dominates, the structure of their societies. But for millions more, especially in the secular societies of the West, religion is regarded as at best an anachronism, at worst a threat to rational thought and intercultural tolerance. In these post-religious countries, which include most of Europe, Canada, Australia, New Zealand, and, to a lesser degree, the United States, organized religion has been reduced to a largely ceremonial role. Serious interest in theology is confined to priests and academics. Yet when questioned, most nonreligious people profess to still believe in "something," although they are not quite sure what. And this is no surprise. Anthropologists maintain that all ancient cultures had some form of belief in gods or a spiritual realm or an afterlife. Clearly some deeply rooted aspect of the human psyche, presumably a product of evolution, compels us to yearn for something that transcends the daily toil and hurly-burly of modern living, a desire to position our lives in something deeper, even cosmic. We like to feel that we mere mortals are part of a grander scheme of things.

The history of religion over the past three centuries is very much a retreat in the face of scientific advancement to the point where science and atheism tend to go hand-in-hand. Yet many scientists share with Einstein a reverence for the beauty and intelligibility of nature, what Einstein himself called a "cosmic religious feeling." Can these vague notions and feelings be sharpened into a concept of God that is thoroughly consistent with science but nevertheless serve what we might call the innate spiritual dimension of human nature?

For adherents of the monotheistic religions, the word *God* traditionally had a very specific meaning, referring to a sort of Cosmic Magician who has always existed, who brought the universe into being from nothing at some specific moment in the past by a supernatural act, and who intervenes from time to time in the great sweep of history and perhaps in day-to-day affairs. Indeed, the Cosmic Magician is still the image of God in much of popular religion today. Needless to say, invoking a miracle-working deity to explain the world does not play out well with scientists. For that matter, it does not play out well with many serious theologians either, whose concept of God is much more abstract but also more remote. In the words of John Robinson, the Anglican bishop of Woolwich in the 1960s and author of *Honest to God*, Christian theologians have shifted their belief from a God "up there" to a God "out there" to what Paul Tillich calls "the ground of being"—that which timelessly sustains physical existence and transcends time and space.

Physicists and cosmologists, familiar as we are with abstract mathematical laws and subtle concepts of reality, have little quarrel with a God that is simply a guarantor of physical laws, considered by many scientists as the ontological soil in which the order found in nature is rooted. Indeed, one can argue that the abstract transcendent God that emerged from classical Christian theology is a natural completion of the reductionist program begun by science.

In a nutshell, reductionism is a line of reasoning that explains the world in terms of smaller and simpler components. Its crowning achievement is atomism, according to which all matter is composed of simple building blocks (atoms) and all change results from the rearrangement of atoms. Today, this basic story has been elaborated to include subatomic particles and dark matter particles, but the reasoning remains the same. Conventional explanations of natural phenomena point downward, to a bottom level of reality, to indecomposable building blocks obeying simple, universal mathematical laws. For most scientists, the buck stops there. That is, the fundamental laws of physics themselves are accepted without explanation. They just *are*. But classical monotheism stands ready with an explanation: the laws are the free creation of an intelligent designer God. Spinoza expressed it clearly: "Now, as nothing is necessarily true save only by Divine decree, it is plain that the universal laws of nature are decrees of God following from the necessity and perfection of the Divine nature. . . . [N]ature, therefore, always observes laws and rules which involve eternal necessity and truth, although they may not all be known to us, and therefore she keeps a fixed and immutable order." In this scheme, God stands at the base of a pyramid, timelessly upholding the laws of the universe, which in turn facilitate and regulate all physical phenomena, including life and consciousness. Most scientists, however, fail to see the necessity for the bottom layer of the pyramid, being content with accepting the laws as given. This standard position is well expressed by the cosmologist Sean Carroll: "At the end of the day the laws are what they are . . . that's okay. I'm happy to take the universe just as we find it." In this argument between science and religion, theologians often justify using God to complete the reductionist explanation of existence by appealing to simplicity. It is simpler, they say, to posit an omnipotent being that creates the universe and its laws than to suppose a package of marvels that just happens to exist reasonlessly.

One shortcoming with a reduction to simplicity, whether invoked by scientists or theologians, is that it appeals to only one mode of investigation into the nature of the physical world. A counter to reductionism is known as *emergence*, and over the past few decades (though the basic concept is much older) it has assumed an increasing importance in science as it has turned more and more toward the study of complexity. But despite its impact on the scientific method, hard-nosed reductionists dismiss emergence, sometimes derisively, as fanciful mumbo-jumbo. A single example will suffice to illustrate the issue. No atom of my body is alive, yet I am alive. The phenomenon of "living" is consistent with, but not reducible to, atomic and molecular interactions. Rather, at each level of material complexity, new qualities that are simply meaningless at lower levels, *emerge* and can be studied in their own right as fundamental phenomena. New laws and regularities emerge with them. Thus life, intelligent behavior, and social complexity can all be seen as emerging from their simpler antecedents and being just as real in their own way as atoms and molecules. Or so claim emergentists. Accepting their position for now, an interesting question arises. Does this hierarchy of complexity and emergence stop with life or social systems? Could there be yet higher levels of emergence?

Until now, emergence has made little impact on theology, and it is this gap that Nancy Abrams sets out to fill in a hugely ambitious project presented in the chapters to follow. In one of the clearest expositions of the power of the emergence concept that I have read, she argues that emergent phenomena and their laws possess genuine ontological status, i.e., they are just as real as the molecules that compose the systems concerned. Her position is captured succinctly in the following paragraph:

> Emergent phenomena like the media and the economy have immense influence on our lives and minds—immeasurably more than does the expansion of the distant universe, which no astronomer doubts is real. Powerful emergent phenomena need to be experienced as *real*. The only alternative is to see them as nothing in themselves—just a lot of individual people doing stuff. But if emergent phenomena are not real, then we have to deny our own existence, because we large animals *are* emergent phenomena. We emerged from clumps of cells, and they emerged from elementary particles, with many levels of emergence in between.

The core of Abrams's extension into theology is that an emergent God can be just as real as, say, the human mind. Because an emergent God is a product of complexity, as opposed to the ultimate ground of being underpinning the rational order of the cosmos, her concept of God contrasts with that of classical theology, though it has some of the elements of process theology (in which a creator God is not absolute and immutable but evolves over time with the universe). Abrams's God is not the grand architect of the cosmos beloved by monotheists but, in fact, a product of the human mind and human society. "God is an ever-growing being yet exists only because of us," she writes. It is an idea the germ of which took root in her mind as a teenager. She describes eight tedious years at Sunday school after which she wrote in a confirmation class essay that shocked her rabbi, "God didn't create us; we created God."

Atheists often argue that God is indeed a product of the human mind and is therefore *not* real. But Abrams came to the conclusion that this simple inversion of traditional belief is too trite.

Recognizing that the concept of emergence offers an entirely new approach to the nature of reality, she realized that an emergent God need not be created by anybody. The core of her bold challenge to the atheist position is that because emergent phenomena can be real in their own right, even if they depend on a lower-level substrate to instantiate them, a God that is the product of the human mind and human society can also be real. After all, life emerges from, and is dependent on, the chemical substrate of organic matter, and life is not only real but has its own (emergent) agenda consistent with, but transcending, the chemical substrate that hosts it. So too can it be for an emergent God. In assembling her case, Abrams draws on her deep understanding of physics, cosmology, and biology and reliably presents ideas from the forefront of those disciplines.

Abrams's deity is not the creator of the universe and not so much the architect of nature as a product of nature—specifically, of human nature. Her God is not even cosmic but planetary, being tied (until now at least) to our particular terrestrial species. Is this not a comedown for those used to envisaging God as the timeless and immutable King of the Universe? Yes and no. For those steeped in traditional monotheism, a God that springs solely from the collective human intellect seems like heresy. But for those who reject the idea of God entirely as ridiculous and superfluous, an emergent God holds many attractions. As Abrams explains, it offers a path to a meaningful human life without coming into conflict with science. It gives humans a "common ground" and introduces something sacred into a generally secular view of nature. In short, it can serve as a focus for the vague spiritual yearnings of our post-religious society.

The success of Abrams's project will depend on how human society copes with the challenges of the coming decades—political, economic, and technological. She makes a case that there is an urgent need for a unifying conceptual framework that can embrace the finest traditions of the ancient religions but move on from them and, in particular, incorporate a scientific world view without relinquishing the spiritual aspects of our humanity. Is this possible? Is an emergent God the way forward for mankind in these troubled times? Abrams's ideas will spark a fresh debate among theologians and scientists. I hope it will inject a new dimension in the stale bickering between atheistic scientists and religious fundamentalists. And in the spirit of the theme that underpins this book, that very debate will itself shape the God that will emerge.

∞

PAUL DAVIES is a world-renowned astrophysicist and cosmologist and is director of the Beyond Center for Fundamental Concepts in Science, Arizona State University. He has made major contributions to understanding how to combine general relativity with quantum mechanics and is the author of almost thirty books, including *Quantum Fields in Curved Space* and popular works such as *The Mind of God, About Time, How to Build a Time Machine, The Fifth Miracle, The Goldilocks Enigma,* and *The Eerie Silence.* He is the winner of many prizes, including the 1995 Templeton Prize, the 2001 Kelvin Medal from the UK Institute of Physics, and the 2002 Michael Faraday Prize from the Royal Society.

INTRODUCTION

For most of my life, a God that was "real" seemed a contradiction in terms. Every idea of God I had ever encountered seemed either physically impossible or so vague as to be empty. I was an atheist married to a famous scientist. But a time came when I needed a higher power. I was forced to acknowledge that, but I didn't know if it would be possible for me. I have no interest in a God that has to be believed in. If I am going to have God in my life, it has to be a God that cannot help but exist, in the same way that matter and gravity and culture exist. We don't need to believe in these things; they just *exist*. We can choose to learn more about them, or not.

I have had the extraordinary privilege of a ringside seat for one of the greatest scientific revolutions in human history. For thirty-eight years I have been married to a man who studies the entire universe as a single evolving entity. My husband, Joel Primack, studies cosmology, the branch of astrophysics that researches the origin, nature, and evolution of the universe. In the early 1980s my then-young husband and three collaborators proposed a theory to solve the great mystery of why there are galaxies. After all, if the Big Bang was symmetrical in all directions, why isn't the universe just a bigger soup? What caused galaxies and clusters of galaxies to form?

Their new theory challenged the assumption that everything is made of atoms. It postulated that the vast majority of matter in the universe is in fact *not* made of atoms or even made of the parts of atoms. It's something completely different, something invisible, called cold dark matter. The theory calculates how the peculiar behavior of cold dark matter could have created the galaxies over time. It was a daring theory, making specific predictions in a field that had scarcely any believable evidence. Some astronomers dismissed it as wildly improbable, but my husband and his collaborators kept developing it with increasing success, realizing a few years later that the other key actor in the evolution of the universe was the even more mysterious "dark energy." That's the energy making the universe expand faster and faster. To test the theory countries around the world have built great observatories on the ground and in space. After three decades the evidence is overwhelming and still pouring in—and it confirms the theory without a single discrepancy. As unlikely as it seemed at first, even to my skeptical husband and his colleagues, the "double dark" theory, based on dark matter and dark energy, has now become accepted in astronomy as the foundation of the modern picture of the universe.

For me a God that is real has to be real not in our commonsense world but in the double dark universe, where we now know we live.

The double dark theory tells a big piece of our origin story. For thousands of years and in virtually all cultures, people have told origin stories, but this is the first one to be based on science and therefore the first origin story in the history of humanity that may actually be accurate. The story is not what anyone, not even Einstein, expected. We're living in a stranger universe than earlier generations ever dreamed. The implications of this discovery for intelligent beings are almost entirely unknown, but inevitably they will be life changing. We have a new picture of the universe. What does a new picture of our universe mean for who *and what* we are?

And what does it mean for God?

The modern world is certainly confused about God. Surveys consistently find that about 90 percent of Americans, and a somewhat smaller majority of people in many other countries, say quite definitely that they believe in God. But when they are asked to explain what they mean by *God*, they become less certain, and there's much divergence of opinion. Is God something authoritarian or supportive, engaged or distant, physical or in the heart? Some describe God as all knowing, all loving, all wise, a careful planner—an entity embodying human characteristics raised to perfection—that created and controls the entire universe, including alien worlds where there could be intelligent creatures with little resemblance to humans. Some believe there is no law of physics an all-powerful God could not break.

Religion's opponents jump in and claim that God does not exist, end of story. This claim is understandable: abuses in the name of religion provide plenty of temptation to feel that the human race might be better off abolishing the whole idea of religion. From this perspective God is at best a fantasy and a distraction, and there are saner and more useful ways to contribute to society.

There was a time when I felt this way.

I remember sitting in Sunday school when I was in the second grade, reading a picture book that showed God as an old bearded man sitting on a cloud and giving orders. I thought, of course *that* couldn't be real! I watched clouds all the time, and I never saw anyone up there. Metaphor was quite beyond me as a child. I took things literally, and then I made my own judgment, which would always seem like the obvious conclusion. The greatest mystery to me as a child was how grown-ups could believe the religious stories they were teaching us. Did they really? Were they crazy or were they intentionally tricking us? The implications either way were confusing. I suffered through eight years of Sunday school. When I was fifteen, the rabbi had my confirmation class write an essay on our personal view of God. "God didn't create us; we created God," I wrote, honestly concluding that God was a fiction invented by weak or illogical people for reasons of convenience or comfort. The rabbi ordered me into his office and yelled at me. "Who do you think you are," he railed, "to question the wisdom of your ancestors?" It was more than a decade before I entered a synagogue again.

When I was an undergraduate at the University of Chicago, I majored in the history and philosophy of science. I studied physics historically, from Thales and Aristotle to Einstein, and was convinced that, though paradigms change, our best chance at truth is through the scientific method. But I also attended lectures by the legendary mythologist and historian of religions Mircea Eliade—if I was lucky enough to hear about them, because he followed no schedule. Eliade was always disappearing for weeks or months, rumor held, to be initiated into the secret shamanic rites of some exotic culture. With his penetrating eyes and ever-present pipe, he was the most intriguing person I had ever met. He seemed to have access to a level of intense existence I had never experienced or even known about. Nor, as far as I could tell, had anyone I had ever encountered in my suburban life. How could his world mesh with the quantum mechanics I was also studying? College gave me my overriding purpose in life: to try to see the big picture—not only the universe and the history of how humans had come to know it but also the deep invisible possibilities of the human, including me.

I became a lawyer and worked for a European environmental-law think tank and later in the science office of Congress, the Office of Technology Assessment. I was fascinated by the connection between science and other realms of human thought, feeling, and ambitions. I saw how vital science is to the decisions that influence our lives yet soon also came to see how little the powerful understand it. Meanwhile I ate for emotional reasons; my weight was out of control. I was always dieting and silently yelling at myself for not doing it right.

Eventually I married and moved to California. I had a successful life teaching, consulting, writing, and raising a young daughter with my husband, but in the privacy of my mind I was brutally self-critical. My good life felt contaminated by guilt and shame stemming from eating and body image. It seemed that half my brain was constantly hounding me about what I could eat, what I shouldn't eat, and what an idiot I was for having eaten whatever I had just eaten. It was a huge effort to accomplish anything, because my focus was constantly interrupted by self-flagellating thoughts. The mental torment was worse by far than the weight.

When my daughter was eight, I found a group of people who were recovering from eating disorders with what they called a spiritual program. They had my problem but they were no longer eating compulsively, and I desperately envied the peace of mind they seemed to have. They said anyone could recover, but I learned to my bewilderment that their program required a "higher power." I was resistant. How could an atheist like me find a higher power believable enough to enable me to do what I had never been able to do on my own? The likelihood of this approached zero. Naive people, I told myself, might believe in higher powers but not me. Although I had been intrigued by mythologies since college, I had never taken the idea of God seriously. It was really hard for me to keep an open mind about such an abused and misused idea as God.

And yet I experienced the first period in my life when food was not a problem. The way of thinking that the program presented gave me a ray of hope for a kind of freedom I had not even imagined possible. A way of life existed that bypassed all the self-flagellating thoughts of diets and self-image, of secret pain and grim determination to lose weight quickly. This new way of life required that I treat myself with love. How hard could that be? Very hard, it turned out, because it was all based on finding a higher power. It always came back to that.

No one could explain to me how this higher power worked or what it was, but with no other option I followed the program's instructions and *imagined* turning my food decisions over to a higher power. I tried to act as if I believed in a higher power, as they suggested. I spoke to some part of my mind as if it were separate, even though it wasn't, and found that doing so was surprisingly worthwhile. I had no illusion that I was talking to anything outside myself. Rather, I realized, I was thinking of the higher power as a loving but unbullshitable witness to my thoughts. It's what I wished I were. Imagining what such a witness would say focused me. I found my consciousness less disposed to denial and self-deceit, more honest, and more courageous. My eating habits greatly improved. I was happier. I got along better with everybody. Some aspect of my consciousness was clearly a better controller of my behavior than my default consciousness, and when I addressed that aspect as my higher power, I was somehow able to conjure up that consciousness and strengthen it in me.

I kept wondering what I was doing, trying to figure it out. At last I decided that the higher power was simply my own best thinking, my higher self, the part I like to have in control. The moment I concluded this, however, I began to sabotage myself. It was as though I realized that, if my higher power was inside me, it could fall under my control. I lost my ability to turn decisions over to it. I was back to square one. I realized it couldn't be inside me, but it couldn't be outside either. I had no answer.

I watched members of the group face terrible life events without desperation. They credited to God their—to me astonishing—ability to accept what they couldn't change and change what they could. They thought of their higher power as God, and it was absolutely clear that their belief in God benefited them. Could the benefits of their kind of faith be inaccessible to people like me who didn't, and wouldn't, believe in a traditional God? I wondered.

Put another way, why should survival benefits go preferentially to those who don't face reality? That seemed to violate the principle of survival of the fittest. I couldn't see how emotional benefits so absolutely fundamental to human success could require belief in God, because those benefits were probably older than the gods. There had to be another way to access them. I was driven to find out. I desperately needed the ability to accept what I could not change and the courage to change what I could.

Twelve-step programs refer to God as "God as we understood Him." Putting aside the masculine pronoun, at first I took this as an admirable statement that people of all religions or none could work the program. Anybody's view of God is okay—just have one. But later I began to see that "God as we understood Him" is not only a basket big enough to accept all ready-made concepts; it's a *challenge* to each of us to find an understanding of God. We commit to try. *Trying to understand* is the point.

I got the sinking feeling that as long as I held on to my unexamined opinions about God, I wouldn't be able to try. Yet I had no other choice but misery.

That was a turning point. I became willing to try. Everything changed. I used to wear eye makeup, but for almost a year I found myself crying too often and had to stop. Life suddenly felt raw, unpolished, like finding a shockingly large diamond in the rough. It wasn't pretty, and yet I saw its potential for me. The willingness to try forced me to start listening differently. It forced me to stop jumping to conclusions when I heard God-talk and instead try to look past the religious metaphors so I could hear what people were struggling to say. I was at the absolute beginning of a long road, but I was—for the first time—facing in the right direction.

I felt committed to find a higher power *of my own understanding*, but I had no idea how to do this. Neither, it seemed to me, did anyone else.

Back home I was watching the double dark universe emerge through my husband's research and that of many other scientists around the world. They were working out the recipe for the entire universe, discovering its ingredients in their proper proportions. It turns out that everything astronomers have ever observed with telescopes and other instruments detecting every wavelength of radiation—all the stars, planets, glowing gas clouds, and dust inside our galaxy, plus all the billions of distant galaxies—totals *less than half of 1 percent* of what's actually out there. Another 4 percent is atoms, mostly hydrogen and helium gas, out between the galaxies, unlit by stars. But 95 percent of the density of the universe consists of those two great moving presences, dark matter and dark energy. They are invisible, not because no light is shining on them but because they *don't interact* with light. The strange and ongoing dance between them, hidden in the background of the visible universe, has spun the galaxies into being and is flinging them away from each other as the universal expansion accelerates.

I was following developments, going to the conferences, meeting the scientists, privy to mysteries of the universe that virtually no one else but the experts knew. I was doing metaphysical insider trading. I paid attention to who was working on alternative versions of the details and what it might mean if this team rather than that one turned out to be right. No civilization has ever tested a view of the universe the way these scientists were.

My recent experience of a greater, more confident self was teaching me something about how my mind works, and cosmology was teaching me how the universe works, and I knew they had to be coherent, since my mind is part of the universe and the concept of a universe is part of my mind. But this was an intellectual, logical conclusion. It didn't *feel* coherent. They were like two perfect halves of a tunnel that fail to meet.

Not a day passed that I did not wonder what in this universe made it possible for my *experience* of a higher power to change me. At a certain point I knew that conjuring up my unbullshitable witness would be my practice for life because it was so effective, even though I did not understand why it worked. But this made me feel even more strongly that I had to figure it out.

At the same time I was realizing that the double dark universe would reverberate far beyond science. *This is the first truly scientific picture of the universe ever*. It will be amended and perhaps encompassed by an even larger theory, but it will not be overthrown. This is our universe. Since the time of Isaac Newton, we've understood how the planets orbit the sun in our own solar system, but our galaxy and almost all the universe beyond have been mystery cloaked in extrapolation. I kept wondering, what does it mean for us humans that we're not living in the kind of universe we thought we were in? Could "God" mean something different in the so-far-unexplored possibilities of this new universe? The one thing I knew for sure was that the only way God can be real is to be real in this new understanding of our very old universe.

My husband and I talked endlessly. How could we communicate the double dark picture to nonscientists? How could we put it into some kind of meaningful context? One of the scariest but most effective ways to learn something difficult is to try teaching it to someone skeptical, so for ten years the two of us cotaught a course at the University of California, Santa Cruz, which we called Cosmology and Culture. It was an attempt to communicate nonmathematically the new picture of the universe—in the context of earlier pictures of the universe from Egypt and Sumer to modern times. The history tells us that earlier changes in cosmology were extremely rare, but when they happened they were accompanied by major changes in the surrounding culture. What may happen as modern scientific cosmology is absorbed into global culture? Each year we tried to break through more effectively. We saw students light up as they realized that the emerging new science could actually answer ancient questions: Where do we come from? What are we made of? Where are we going?

Together my husband and I wrote two books, *The View from the Center of the Universe* and *The New Universe and the Human Future*, to help readers wrap their minds around the new picture of the universe and get some sense of its relevance to us humans. We traveled around the world, giving more than a hundred talks at universities, bookstores, international conferences, astronomy clubs, forums, churches, even the US Treasury. Almost everyone is fascinated by the idea of a new understanding of our universe. It has repercussions for politics, economics, and even the ways we live our daily lives and define what we are as human beings.

One thing our books did not discuss was God. Nevertheless we received many e-mails from readers who had profound spiritual reactions to our books. I found these e-mails deeply moving: so many people wanted to know where God fit in this new universe. But I had no answer.

The truth is that I wasn't ready to talk about God. Privately I was still on my quest to learn the source of the power and comfort and inspiration that the idea of a higher power offers. I wanted to visualize that source through the lens of a reality that's based not on wishful thinking or tradition but on evidence—not only from cosmology but also biology, psychology, neuroscience, the study of complexity, and the history of religion and culture. After so many years of feeling torn apart, I wanted to *feel coherent* intellectually, emotionally, and spiritually. I wanted a spiritual practice consistent with everything I know. I longed to be at peace with myself.

And then one day it hit me: I didn't have to work from some prepackaged idea of "God" and ask if that could exist. The question "Does God exist?" is a hopeless distraction that will never lead anywhere positive. I had to turn the fundamental question on its head. If I wanted to find a God that is real, I had to start from what's real, what actually exists. I realized that the question that matters is this: *Could anything actually exist in the universe, as science understands it, that is worthy of being called God?*

If the answer to my question is yes, then this is a huge discovery. It means that those of us who feel conflicted or even intellectually dismissive about a traditional kind of God, but who long for some spiritual connection, can enjoy the benefits of a genuine higher power in our lives, open-heartedly.

This shift in approach was like waking from a dream. Suddenly coherence became possible, because from a cosmic perspective the answer to my question became *yes*. Yes, there is something that truly fulfills the need for God and is also consistent with a cutting-edge scientific outlook.

If we give this idea a serious chance—if we can tamp down the usual reflex of resistance—this way of thinking about God can be comforting, awe inspiring, empowering, and in harmony with science.

That's what this book is about.

The thing is, the new universe is counterintuitive in several ways, and therefore so is what it allows to be possible. To open our minds to this new understanding of God, we have to be clear about what God can't be—in *this* universe, at least. And to liberate the mind to accept what God can't be, it really helps to appreciate how ideas about God have always been changing. These are the subjects of the first two chapters. In chapter 3, I'll be able to talk about what a real God could be.

And in the rest of the book I will look at the far-flung implications.

If only everyone could relax, even for a moment, the taboo around questioning God. If only everyone could, for one shining moment, act as if this new idea were true—try it out by moving in with all their furniture, the way scientists are willing to live inside a theory as if it's true, sometimes for years, in order to test it and discover its implications. For those who are willing to do this, I don't think it's an exaggeration to say it will transform your life. It has mine.

I have written this book because what began as a personal quest for a higher power that could free me from food addiction has blossomed into something larger than me. My discoveries may be useful to anyone who is dissatisfied with worn-out images and tired liturgies about God but is unwilling to dismiss the quest for spiritual insight. They are for anyone who is sick of the battle between religion and science, which generally pits a caricature of religion against a caricature of science and, not surprisingly, seems never to progress.

That battle cannot be resolved within the current popular state of knowledge. We have to go beyond that state to find the resolution—and for the first time the knowledge is becoming available that makes it possible. This book is a journey into the heart of the new scientific universe—the heart, that is, in the sense of those aspects of the universe that touch our core as human beings.

Because in that *connection* between the new universe and ourselves lies the key to a God that could be real.

We've all grown up so steeped in tradition, whether we've accepted it or rebelled against it, that it's hard to grasp that the chance to *redefine* God is actually in our hands. But it is, and the way we do it will play a leading role in shaping the future of civilization. The good news is that we no longer have to do it by compulsion, tradition, or reflex. We can start rethinking our understanding of God in light of knowledge we never had before. We humans are participants in a cosmic venture: the multibillion-year evolution of complex intelligent life from nothing but particles and energy. The way we define God can either bless this extraordinary cosmic venture or slowly choke it to death.

It's time to stop struggling with traditional views of God—struggling with each other as well as within our own minds. All the old views of God are demonstrably inadequate to our times. They perpetuate conflict or fail to inspire us enough to rise to the existential challenges of our complex world. That religion is today seen as separate from everything else is a sure sign that it is not about our real lives but about an image that some people are trying to impose on sprawling, unpredictable reality.

How we think about God matters enormously, and the dawn of a new cosmology is the best opportunity we may ever have to get it right. If we dare to let God be real in this universe, we may actually come to understand aspects of God, as well as feel the intimacy that real presence provides. *If we look for God in what is real*, the argument about God's existence is over, and we can begin to learn its true nature and relationship to us. We can begin to experience our special place, and God's, in the dynamism of the double dark cosmos.

Today many people, including powerful leaders, are turning to their religious traditions for principles to guide their decision making, but no religion has any experience with truly large-scale problems. The great religions were designed to confront only a tiny subset of what happens in our lives today. Each of us has to deal not only with our extended family, our community, and the natural world but also with thousands of strangers, languages, international news, entertainment, insidious advertising, and the entire Internet. And the reality of all of us doing this at once generates global markets and economies, nations, networks, and civilizations. Our worlds are more complicated by many orders of magnitude than those of the peoples who created our traditional ideas of God. We need to *discover* the principles that govern affairs on these immensely more complex scales. They can't be intuited, and they can't be derived from simpler thinking. None of our religions or political ideologies borne of narrower worlds can guide the future of humanity.

But something can.

While today's dominant mind-sets about God are tearing us apart, both internally and from each other, the real God silently waits. For most of my life I never thought of God as part of the salvation of our species. I didn't even see what I needed for my own salvation. But I have changed and so can anyone. I'm not trying to convince you to see God exactly as I do. I am simply offering my discovery. I am laying out what science has revealed to me and how I made sense of it. From this new perspective we can start, if we choose, to experience our unbreakable blood bond with Earth and with our grandparent, the cosmos. If we rethink God in light of this new knowledge, it may help us humans to find the wisdom and bravery we need to face our future together.

What I have learned is this: Having no spiritual life at all is like never really falling in love. Developing a spiritual bond with a *fantasy* is like falling in love with someone who will never love you back. But developing a spiritual bond with *the real universe* is like falling in love with someone who is already in love with you. That's where God is.

A GOD THAT COULD BE REAL

PART I

CHAPTER 1

God Evolves

We live in an expanding universe, and in an expanding universe everything is moving. Nothing stands still across time. What is real evolves. The changing ideas of God that I discuss in this chapter are limited to those that developed into the Judeo-Christian traditions, but similar evolutions have happened in all spiritual traditions. The irony is that ideas only become "traditions" after they've been changed countless times by different practitioners' interpretations.

In the ancient Middle East before the development of monotheism, every people had its gods. These gods were not arbitrary spirits but often personifications of the forces of nature—the miraculous, uncontrollable, often frightening, sometimes trivial, and sometimes awe-inspiring powers of the world in which our ancestors found themselves. They named these powers as gods and saw them as having specific characters and histories of interaction, as well as the ability to understand human languages and hearts. Ancient people bound their complex stories of the gods to the movements of the stars and the rhythms of the seasons, which people carefully observed, believing it was their responsibility to the gods to get it right. What these people understood was not what we would consider scientifically accurate today, but their ideas made sense then, given the way people and culture experienced nature. The stories of the gods connected people emotionally to shared meanings hidden inside daily life.

The concept of one god came together gradually. The ancient Hebrews had no sudden, pure, and complete idea of monotheism but rather complex collages, often enriched with polytheistic ideas subtly rephrased and recast.

Nothing stands still across time, but one thing came close: for three thousand years, despite the shifting identities of the gods and the changing languages and demographics of the ancient Middle East, despite the change from polytheism to monotheism, the physical picture of the universe remained essentially unchanged. In that picture the universe consisted of a flat earth beneath a domed sky filled with stars. Beyond—both above and below—lay the cosmic waters. This was the bedrock belief, and no version of the gods contradicted it. In fact, the gods explained it.

Today we have nothing like this—no commitment to model our origin story or understanding of God on the universe *as we understand it today*.

For years, whenever my husband and I encountered a religious leader from any tradition, we would seize the opportunity to ask this question: What difference does it make to your religion that the universe is expanding? We always got more or less the same answer: No difference. The religious leaders found it interesting and perhaps important scientifically, but they did not see how it could change the fact that, *however* the universe operates, God is still God. There was a total disconnect between their picture of God and the universe that they were crediting Him with creating, and they thought this was normal.

It's not normal. We may be the first major culture in history to have a God that is immune to the way the universe is known to operate.

That our popular notions of God do not give us any meaningful connection to our contemporary understanding of the cosmos is a deep but largely unrecognized loss in the modern world. It means that we have no believable big picture of how we and our God fit into the cosmos. The unconscious need to compensate for this loss of meaning may be what propels so many people today into dogma, denial, or distractions.

But it doesn't have to be this way. For the first time we know enough that we can rediscover the sense of integrity and coherence with our universe and our God—if we have the courage to think in a new way. Images of God that are impossible and inadequate to our times dominate millions of people's spiritual lives, and this leads to suspicion not only of people with different images of God but suspicion of science itself. Gods are holding people back. We can reclaim the good that has been lost without compromising the good that has been found in this age of science. We can understand God in a way that serves us in the world we actually live in. This is our moment to move forward.

ANCIENT GODS OF THE FLAT EARTH

In the beginning was the Primeval Water. It was not a sea with a surface but a watery Abyss in all directions, endless, formless, and dark. So began an origin story of ancient Egypt that was as old when the Bible was written as the Bible is today. In the story out of the watery Abyss came Light. Light was both male and female and gave birth to the goddess of Harmony, Order, Law, and the Right Way. Harmony passed her wisdom down through descendant gods and into the future world organically, through birth after birth. Air and Moisture were born and gave birth to Heaven and Earth. Earth was recumbent in all the images of him, and Heaven arched her back over him, her body filled with stars.

What was it like to live with such an understanding of the universe?

Imagine that you are an ancient Egyptian, lying on a hilltop in total darkness on a warm moonless night. A great swath of pale white light crosses the entire sky. That is the Nile, the real Nile, the *Winding Waterway*. The river here on earth that people call the Nile is its reflection.

You lie back and relax into the beauty of the stars. You can feel the presence of their mother, the great goddess Heaven, arching over you as you lie on the warm sweet body of the earth god. Heaven is as huge as the sky. You can feel her protecting you from the forces of chaos beyond. If you look deeply into her, between the stars, you can almost see the world of spirit, the Dwat, ruled by her son Osiris. In the perpetual darkness within the goddess, the sun is traveling on his nightly journey, stripped of his brilliant outward form, being renewed and prepared. The goddess will give birth to him again in the morning and swallow him again at the end of the day. You too were born from the Dwat, and at death you will return. "Oh, my mother," you pray to her, using well-known words carved into the stone of the pyramids, "spread yourself above me so that I can be placed among the unchanging stars and never die."

Egypt had a relatively benign climate—the Nile flooded at the same time every year, predictably fertilizing the farms with rich silt

Figure 1. The ancient Egyptian cosmos: the goddess Nut, who represents the heavens, arches her back over the god Geb, the earth, while their father holds them apart.

and then subsiding to allow another planting—so Water, Light, Air, Moisture, Heaven, and Earth represented the genealogy of the powers that ruled Egypt. But a mere eight hundred miles away in Mesopotamia, nature had a different character. There were scorching winds and torrential storms; the Tigris and Euphrates rivers would rise unpredictably, destroying crops and sometimes entire villages, creating a more pessimistic and resigned mood. So it's not surprising that the two most powerful gods of Sumer, the first great civilization of Mesopotamia, were the male sky god and his violent son, the storm god.

Egypt was a unified kingdom by about 3000 BCE, but Mesopotamia had warring city-states, and the origin story of Babylon involved a war among the gods. The hero was the high god of Babylon, named Marduk, whose fabulously dynamic story is preserved in great detail on still-readable clay tablets. After descending from earlier generations of gods, these tablets tell us, Marduk fought a terrifying battle with the primal goddess of the sea and all her monsters. He killed her with the same weapons that Sumerians millennia earlier had associated with the storm god, showing that the god of Babylon now controlled the most ancient powers. But a look at how Marduk did it reveals several familiar elements. Marduk divided the slaughtered sea goddess (the primeval waters) in two, bolted her upper waters in place, and from her lower half fashioned the earth, mountains, and rivers. He measured carefully—the Babylonians were brilliant astronomical observers—and he set the celestial beings in their places with precisely calculated instructions. At the end of his labors the celebrating gods built the city of Babylon for themselves. Taking the blood of the sea goddess's defeated general—the blood of a loser and a lackey—Marduk created humans to serve the gods by doing all the work so the gods could enjoy their city, whose hanging gardens were one of the wonders of the ancient world.

Both conceptually and emotionally Babylonians lived in a radically different spiritual world from the Egyptians'. Egyptians saw themselves as the direct descendants of the gods, entrusted with the

Figure 2. The biblical flat-earth cosmos.

world, but Babylonians saw themselves as created to be servants of the gods. Yet the physical picture of the universe was exactly the same in Babylon as in Egypt: the earth was a flat pancake with a bubble of air above it, surrounded in all directions forever by the primeval water.

THE ANCIENT HEBREW COSMOS

And the cosmos remained the same for the Hebrews. The only real difference was that the Hebrews didn't see earth, air, sky, and water as gods or as having been made from gods; in monotheism these aspects of nature were inanimate, since there could be only one God.

Imagine that you're a Hebrew shepherd, lying at night on a hillside and tending your sheep. How beautifully the stars are mounted in the firmament. The dome of the heavens is so huge, so solid. Tonight is peaceful, but you wonder what it must have felt like to the people of Noah's time when they saw the dome open and the water slam down and drown every living thing. What astonishing power God must have to build something that could hold up so much water. It gives you

chills to think about it. You can sense the presence of God everywhere
and wonder whether you should be thinking such thoughts. You know
that God walked with Adam in the garden and spoke to Moses on the
mountain, but you can't imagine how this presence could walk or talk.
Did God take a form? No, that's not possible, the very thought violates
the commandment against graven images. You sigh. You think about
the water far below you, below the earth, the water that can never be
seen, and you are glad that God made dry land and gave you sheep.

Nature hadn't changed, but monotheism changed people's ways
of visualizing and explaining nature, requiring new origin stories.
In the beginning, according to Genesis 1, there was nothing but
the eternal God hovering over the "deep." The word *deep* in Hebrew may have been closely related to the Babylonian name of the
sea goddess who was conquered by Marduk. On the first day God
created light, and on the second He, like Marduk, divided the waters, securing the upper waters in the sky, not with a bolt but with
a "hard thing," translated into English two thousand years later in
the King James version as the "firmament." The idea was the same:
something had to hold up the upper waters to provide a bubble of
air in which the Creation would happen. On the third day, according to Genesis, God established dry ground upon the lower waters
and brought forth all the plants. On the fourth He created the sun,
moon, and stars, and on the fifth the creatures of the sea and air. On
the sixth day He created all the land animals and, in His own image,
man and woman together, to whom He gave dominion over the
plants and animals. On the seventh day He rested and thus created
the Sabbath.

Many commentators have offered complicated reasons why
God created plants before the sun, moon, and stars, when everyone
knows plants can't live without sunshine. The simplest explanation
is that this was the order of creation in the Babylonian origin story
and the order of the planetary gods in the Babylonian week. The
agricultural god came third in the week, while the god of astronomy

came fourth. The Genesis storyteller was most likely emphasizing *not that this was the order in which God had historically constructed the universe* but that the nature powers, as the Babylonians defined them, were now claimed by the Hebrew God for himself. The Hebrew God's legitimacy largely rested on His *authority over nature* as it was understood at the time.

The Hebrew obsession with Babylon was not happenstance. Babylon had conquered Jerusalem and taken the leading Jews captive. The Babylonian captivity lasted for several generations until Persia conquered Babylon and allowed Jews to return home. Although the Jews held their own traditional stories sacred, they were a pastoral people and had been greatly influenced by the high urban culture of Babylon. The Torah (the first five books of the Bible) was compiled around 500 BCE, as Jews were returning to Jerusalem. The redactors of the Torah may have been led by Ezra the Scribe. According to Ezra 7, the king of Persia sent Ezra, a Jew, to Jerusalem to codify the law of Moses and encourage the God of heaven to favor the Persian king. The Torah pulled together traditional stories, mainly from four Jewish sources that had been written in different eras. These sources used different names for God and characterized God somewhat differently. The team of redactors cut, pasted, and massaged these often inconsistent texts to produce the codification of law and history that became holy scripture.

In the story of creation in six days, God is calm and majestic, planning each step of the creation of the world and deeming most of it good. But the historically much older story of Adam and Eve, which the redactors decided to place second, portrays God as an emotional being who blows up when disobeyed, then regrets it. The redactors also combined different versions of some stories, for example, Noah and the flood. This is why there are so many inconsistencies, such as the number of each animal on the ark (in one place two of each, male and female, but a few lines later two of the unclean animals and seven of the clean ones, presumably for food). By artistically weaving together many stories, the redactors created a complicated portrait of a God who was inconsistent and unpredictable, even if all powerful, but who could be a God to everyone.

More than two thousand years would pass before historians would figure all this out and realize that it was the process of cutting and pasting that gave God the complicated and changeable personality He appears to have in the Torah. The God of the Hebrew Bible was a new God, a collage of many gods—and not just versions of the monotheistic God. For example, the Bible calls worship of the Canaanite god Baal an abomination, yet many beautiful poetic praises of Baal, which have been found on tablets from the ancient Canaanite city of Ugarit, appear almost word for word in the Psalms as praises of the Hebrew God. Borrowing songs, praises, prophecies, and poetic descriptions from other traditions, changing only the name of the god, was common in the Middle East. The only important question was in whose honor the stories were told and the songs were sung.

This new amalgamated image of God was a challenge to accept. The Genesis 1 idea of creation by a calm omniscient being who has no competitors was not something people of that time could easily understand. Many Hebrews had an emotional need to see God not as having simply created the world alone and unopposed but as having fought hard for victory over the forces of chaos. They wanted their God to have *earned* his place, as Marduk had. Many biblical passages suggest that the Hebrew God had not just ordered inanimate water to divide but in fact had, like Marduk, won a great battle with the Deep and her monsters. "Thou didst divide the sea by thy might; thou didst break the heads of the dragons on the waters. Thou didst crush the heads of Leviathan" (Ps. 74:13–14). "Thou dost rule the raging of the sea; when its waves rise, thou stillest them. Thou didst crush Rahab [a legendary sea monster in the chaos before Creation] like a carcass, thou didst scatter thy enemies with thy mighty arm" (Ps. 89:9–10). "He gathered the waters of the sea as in a bottle; He put the deep in storehouses" (Ps. 33:7). "By his power he stilled the sea; by his understanding he smote Rahab. By his wind the heavens were made fair; his hand pierced the fleeing serpent" (Job 26:10–13). This imagery was the language of polytheism, bubbling up despite valiant efforts by the priests of monotheism to suppress it.

The Hebrews eventually made the leap of faith to monotheism, but even this immense mental transformation made no difference at all to their picture of the universe. Polytheist or monotheist, everyone in the ancient Middle East believed the earth was flat, with water below it, air above, and a water-filled sky held in place by the might of whichever god had brought order from chaos.

THE BIRTH OF SCIENCE SHAKES THE GODS

About the same time that the Torah was being compiled, philosophers in Greece were developing an extraordinarily radical idea: the earth was not flat but a sphere at the center of a spherical universe, and all the celestial objects orbited around it. Most Greeks, however, were not philosophers. To the average Greek dozens of self-serving unpredictable gods were in charge—not only of external events but even of people's own thoughts. Greek gods were believed capable of reaching in and changing your thinking without your even being aware of it. Plato came up with the term *theology* to fight this view because it threatened rationality. He criticized poets, not because he was opposed to beauty but because epic poetry was what spread the mythology of the gods and reinforced their emotional and irrational authority over phenomena. Plato's theology was supposed to be a purely rational approach to the gods (*theos*) through reason (*logos*). Plato never questioned the reality of the gods, only whether what was said about them was the truth.

Greek philosophers invented the concept of cosmos—the order of the universe, which existed *independent of gods*. To the Greek philosophers cosmology was not about crediting the gods but about explaining how things operate. The daring of this approach can hardly be overstated. By seeking natural explanations for phenomena, the Greeks automatically invented the opposite concept of "the supernatural." The natural was an entire realm that they defined, radically, as outside the power of the gods. The peoples of the Middle East drew no clear dividing line between gods and the natural world: the Nile flowed from the spiritual realm onto farms; the Hebrew God created the world with words. Without denying the existence of the gods, the Greek philosophers set limits on the gods' powers.

Rome rose and fell, the Dark Ages passed, and by the high Middle Ages everyone with any education believed, along with the Greek philosophers, that the earth was a sphere at the center of the universe.

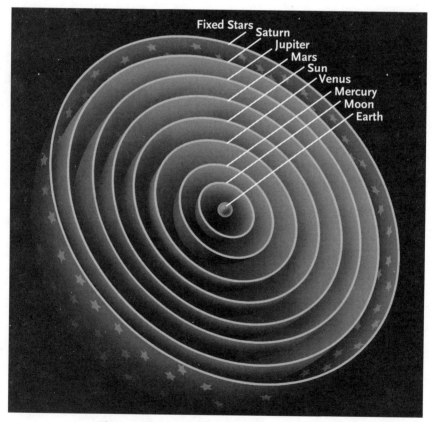

Figure 3. The medieval earth-centered cosmos.

MEDIEVAL SPHERICAL COSMOS

Although Christians in Europe believed the biblical story of creation was literally true, they also believed that the spherical earth was the center of a set of transparent crystal nested spheres, each carrying a planet, the sun, or the moon. These "heavenly spheres" rotated at different rates around the earth, producing the "music of the spheres." The outermost sphere carried the fixed stars, and beyond that lay heaven. In the *Divine Comedy* Dante describes the realm beyond the spheres as "pure light, intellectual light, full of love." It had been a challenge to reconcile the pagan Greek cosmos with the biblical Creation story, but the Catholic Church had had a thousand years to do it.

Imagine it is the year 1200 and you are a monk. You have just awakened in your cell. It is pitch black and very cold, too early to wake the others for morning prayers. You wrap yourself tightly in your woolen cassock and fling open the window. The moon has not yet set. The world outside is silent and the sky sparkles with stars. You shiver, not only with the cold but with the awesome beauty above.

Everything in creation has a place that God has decreed for it, and it moves toward that place by its own desire, because it loves God and wants to fulfill His will. God has given every object this tendency, to keep the universe orderly. Earth is at the center of the universe because it is the heaviest of all elements. The waters lie above it, the air above that, and fire soars upward to the heavens. How nice a fire would be now.

You look up at Jupiter, gleaming brighter than any light but the sun and moon, riding ever so regally upon its crystal sphere below the stars. For the last few nights you've noticed that Saturn is following close behind Jupiter, and Jupiter is chasing the moon, getting closer and closer every night. Everyone knows Saturn brings great misfortune, but he is following on the heels of kingly Jupiter, who brings great fortune. What can this portend? Of course, the planets are not gods. The Romans were unredeemed pagans, and their gods' names on the planets mean nothing. There is only one true God. The planets simply ride their crystal spheres, tracing perfect circles forever around the earth. Still, their influence is so powerful! Last season your sister almost died from something the planets sent through the air. The doctor told her that's what it was. And she wasn't the only one—many people died from the influenza of the planets.

Soon it will be time to wake the other monks for morning prayers. If you all pray at exactly the same moment with all the other monks at all the other monasteries, God will surely hear you. It's a good thing, too—if you had to send prayers to God by mule, and the mule walked forty miles a day straight up past Saturn in the seventh heaven, it would take eight thousand years to get just to the sphere of the fixed stars. What a huge sphere—so big, in fact, you can hardly imagine how it can turn all the way around the earth every day, even with the love of God driving it. And God is even farther away! You can't imagine being that high without feeling physically dizzy. But whenever you walk into the cathedral and look way up at the angels on the ceiling, you do understand, at least a little. No matter how high the sphere of the heavens is, God and the angels are always there looking down at you. Wind gusts in your window, and you pull your woolen cassock more tightly around you.

You can't stop thinking about the strange story you heard last week from the visiting monk, and you feel bewildered. He said that the stars are actually bigger than the earth and all lit by the sun. But, then, what are they? Countless stars, all bigger than the earth, riding around fast on a single sphere. It doesn't make sense. You feel much happier with the explanation you have always known—that the stars are tiny windows in the great sphere, opening onto heaven beyond. What you are seeing at this moment is God's divine light shining through them. He's right there on the other side of the sphere, reaching through to us with his divine light. He has to shield us from most of his light, though, or we would all die. It says so in the Bible. Even Moses had to shield his eyes when God walked by.

You look longingly at the realms of the heavenly spheres. They are filled with angels and other ethereal beings, all overflowing with divine love. The heavens are so much more beautiful than the corrupt earth.

But we each have to live out our time here first, in whatever place God put us, and he has placed us here on earth, in this cold place full of suffering, far outside heaven. The moon is setting. It's time to wake the others for morning prayers. You rub your stiff legs and arms to warm them so you can move. This is your lot in life—to join your voice with those of the other monks so that when you all pray together, God cannot help but hear. Yours is an important role, and you are grateful for it. You close the window and begin your day's work.

By the Middle Ages the polytheism of the ancient world was long gone, but in addition to God, Jesus, Mary, and the saints there were angels and spirits. The planets (the Greek word meant "wanderers in the sky" because they don't move with the stars) were still mysterious beings bearing the names of pagan gods, as did the days of the week (they still do). The planets were not exactly gods, but the crystal spheres that carried them were nevertheless considered intelligent beings that kept turning because they loved God. Monotheism had not killed the personification of forces of nature but had renamed and recast them.

Medieval Christian theologians were masters of disputation, but they were in surprising agreement about one thing: the meaning of the biblical prediction that God would destroy the world with fire. They were certain that it could refer only to the world *beneath* the moon (which was embedded in the innermost crystal sphere) because the heavenly spheres were eternal and therefore God would never destroy them. No one then had any comprehension that the biblical prediction had been written by someone who believed the earth was flat—someone who had never heard of heavenly spheres or considered the problem of whether the wording of the prediction should cover spheres. To the medieval theologians the prediction was scripture. Therefore it was true, and their job was to make sense of it. They had no understanding that ideas of God had changed substantially since biblical times. Until biblical scholarship developed as a field in the nineteenth and twentieth centuries, theologians did not understand that dominant ideas of God were always undergoing a process of unconscious evolution. To the medieval mind God would never conceive of destroying the heavenly spheres. Theologians did their absolute best to make their image of God consistent with the universe *as they understood it at the time.*

AN ERA OF CONFUSION

The Copernican revolution helped end the Middle Ages in Europe and begin the Enlightenment. In the 1500s the Polish astronomer Nicholas Copernicus suggested that astronomers could better calculate the motions of the planets by assuming, theoretically, that the sun, rather than the earth, was the center of the universe. Galileo (1564–1642) then proved with the first telescopic observations of the sky that the heavenly spheres could not be real. Johannes Kepler (1571–1630) figured out that the planets moved not in perfect circles but in elliptical orbits around the sun, and Isaac Newton (1643–1727) figured out the laws of motion and gravity, realizing that the same force that pulls an apple to the ground keeps the planets in their orbits.

For a thousand years people had believed God was physically out there, surrounding the universe with divine light. Suddenly there were no heavenly spheres and never had been. Earth itself, people were told, was moving; it was a planet orbiting the sun, and beyond lay an incomprehensibly vast, shapeless, and mostly empty space, scattered randomly with stars.

Europeans living through this epic shift found it wrenching, almost impossible to take in. The notion that the whole earth was moving simply defied common sense. The sixteenth-century philosopher Jean Bodin wrote, "No one in his senses, or imbued with the slightest knowledge of physics will ever think that the earth, heavy and unwieldy from its own weight and mass, staggers up and down around its own center and that of the sun; for at the slightest jar of the earth, we would see cities and fortresses, towns and mountains thrown down." Martin Luther wrote: "People gave ear to an upstart astrologer who strove to show that the earth revolves, not the heavens or the firmament, the sun and the moon. . . . This fool wishes to reverse the entire science of astronomy, but sacred Scripture tells us that Joshua commanded the sun to stand still, and not the earth." The new scientific picture of the solar system flouted both common sense and religious authority. But it won out because it worked: its predictions were in perfect agreement with observations of tides, eclipses, and the motions of comets, asteroids, the planets, and their moons. The new physics was so empowering that enthusiastic adopters extrapolated its applicability to the entire universe.

The picture of the universe that followed Newton's discoveries in the seventeenth century is the picture that most educated secular people still hold today. It portrays us as living on an average planet of an average star in a cosmos where no place is different from any other; space goes on, perhaps forever; and there is no physical location for God. To science-respecting European Enlightenment thinkers, God no longer needed a physical place and couldn't be described by physical laws. God became an indefinably nonphysical kind of thing. God became supernatural.

Within monotheism God had evolved from a deity whose legitimacy came from taking over the powers of nature to a deity vague enough not to have to interact with nature at all.

This was the beginning of the profound *incoherence* between our spiritual lives and our physical reality. Today the great majority of Americans in every poll say they believe in God. But according to a Baylor University survey, when they are pushed to explain what they mean, more than 25 percent of those who call themselves believers don't actually believe in a personal God but rather a "distant God" that's not active in the modern world. These people lead secular lives. They think of God as a cosmic force that set the laws of nature in motion and then disappeared. They have adopted an idea of God that serves no purpose whatsoever in their lives except to prevent them from appreciating how the universe actually began.

The separation of God from nature began four centuries ago. Since then countless professional theologians and others have attempted to make sense of a God who exists in Newtonian placelessness. But something essential has been lost.

In ancient Egypt the god Osiris was the constellation Orion, and Isis was the brightest star in the sky, Sirius, always at Orion's right hand. Since people of that time made no distinction between physical and spiritual worlds, they felt they could actually see these gods in the night sky. Every temple and pyramid was precisely oriented to the stars. In every way they could think of, these ancient people tied their understanding of their world and their gods to the cosmos, and their civilization lasted three thousand years. They understood something we need to relearn: that the cosmos is the most stable foundation that God, then or now, can ever have, because the cosmos is what we believe reality to be. It was, after all, the experience of the powers of nature that evoked the first gods. Gods that have nothing to do with the real world have ultimately no foundation but hearsay.

The only stable foundation for God, then or now, is the cosmos—but that means the cosmos *as the culture best understands it.*

From these distant ancestors we can begin to see what we need to do to incorporate and synchronize our ideas of God with our universe and find a deep sense of truth, comfort, and empowerment. Our ancestors sought harmony with the universe. We can, too.

Modern culture has not absorbed the twenty-first-century scientific picture yet, but it will. That the new picture of the universe does not eliminate God should help smooth its acceptance.

BRINGING GOD INTO THE MODERN COSMOS

What links so many of history's wildly different ideas under the name *God*? Why do we hold on to this concept? If we could answer these questions, we could zero in on the essence of God rather than on overused traditional God images that function by now like blinders on a horse.

I am arguing that the idea of God has persisted through thousands of years and thousands of cultural changes neither because God is an independently existing being in control of the universe nor because it's a purely psychological need. God persists and always will because it's a *fundamental characteristic of the connection* between ourselves and the universe. That we're connected to the universe is inevitable and indisputable, but until we had a scientific understanding of the universe, we could not imagine *how*. Now we have such an understanding, at least in outline, so we can break out of the old metaphors for God that have so cramped our thinking and expectations.

It matters enormously to understand that ideas of God have evolved and are continuing to evolve. With no comprehension of this, religious communities have often imposed severe punishments on those who dare to question what is, in fact, a momentary view of God—a single frame in a movie thousands of years long. Gradually every long-lived religious tradition has diverged into multiple versions. There are hundreds of official ways to be Christian. Muslims are still fighting with each other about centuries-old disputes. Even demographically tiny Judaism has split into at least five major movements and several smaller ones. In each subset of these belief systems, a somewhat different version of God's character and expectations of us is held not only to be true for the believers but to be *universally and eternally true*. The accusation of blasphemy is not so powerful in democracies anymore, although it can be in other countries with other forms of government, but in some religious communities, even in democracies, speaking profanely or incorrectly about God is still viewed with suspicion and even hostility.

So it seems that the *unconscious* evolution of ideas about God is inevitable, but to evolve God *consciously* is frightening and unacceptable.

This has to change. There is nothing to fear.

A new picture of cosmic reality doesn't overturn everything at once. It doesn't mean that morality will break down or change at a faster rate. But it does mean that we are free to look at the evidence and ask ourselves what the possibilities are for God in this universe.

Today's cosmological revolution is exploding the old ideas of reality. For the first time we can *accurately* see our cosmic context. We have enough historical and scientific knowledge to openly and consciously participate in the evolution of God. Doing so matters—certainly far more than I ever imagined before I began this spiritual odyssey—because the idea of God has power we will need. Something about God is real to most humans. It's larger than our individual lives and can make us thrive or suffocate. So what is the best way to think about it? How can it help us to thrive? How can we make the next stage in the evolution of God a positive one for ourselves and our descendants for generations to come?

We can welcome the universe as it is being revealed, and we can come to love and appreciate our special place in it. We're immersed in it, and its history lives on inside our bodies and brains, as I'll explain in subsequent chapters. We can use new scientific knowledge and abilities to help us come much closer to reality—as close as is possible in our era—rather than closet ourselves in fantasies that blind us to the miracle that surrounds us and fills us. By opening our minds to the best knowledge of our time, we can come to visualize God as real and integral to the universe. And it will still be God, still there for us. We can meld our spirituality intimately into the new cosmos.

When no one knew what the universe was, there could be alternative beliefs, but now we know. Pretending we don't simply because the truth seems weird or inconvenient or doesn't feel right will force us to shut down our minds and straightjacket our ability to experience the natural world. It will stunt our children, sabotage what may be their best tools, and shrink their chances of dealing successfully with the global problems they are inheriting. And it will throw away an opportunity for our species that may never come again: the opportunity to *re-envision our connection with the universe*. Only if we demand that God be real can we have God and also live in cosmic reality. And cosmic reality is the only place our species—or God—can survive. Cosmic reality is the only place we can become coherent in our minds, our hearts, our behavior, and our visions for the future.

We have the opportunity to do what our ancestors never realized anyone could do: take a creative, active role in the evolution of God.

CHAPTER 2

A God That Can't Be Real

Science can never tell you with certainty what's true, since there's always the possibility that some future discovery will rule it out. But science can often tell you with certainty what's not true. Galileo, for example, showed with telescopic evidence that the heavenly spheres could not exist, even though he could not actually prove that Earth moves around the sun. When scientists produce the evidence that convincingly rules out the impossible, there's no point in arguing. It's over. Grace lies in accepting and recalculating. That's how science moves forward.

What if we thought this way about God? What if we took the evidence of a new cosmic reality seriously and became willing to rule out the impossible? What if we cleared away those distracting notions of God that can't be true in the kind of universe we actually live in? God can be imagined to do or be anything, but the goal of this book is to find a God that is real.

It's amazing how many unnecessary requirements have gotten tacked onto God. Unnecessary requirements are harmful. They divide us from each other, since different people see them differently; worse, they divide us from our own rational selves. A religion that credits God with powers that can't exist in this universe sets its followers up for inevitable doubt, which in turn requires of them an exhausting effort to jack up their faith in order to fight the evidence against it. This is self-sabotage. People are expending all that effort and worry to defend "characteristics" of God that no one really needs.

So here's a chance to pare our definition of God down to the essentials.

In my quest for a believable higher power, I decided to look one by one at the reasons God seemed unbelievable and ask if they really matter or whether they are merely traditional attributes. The results of this exercise amazed me.

Not one characteristic that conflicts with science turns out to *matter*. We can let them go.

Shakespeare said it best in *Richard II*: "Superfluous branches we lop away that bearing boughs may live." Here are the branches that must be lopped away that a real God may live. These beliefs can't be literally true in our universe. To the extent we cling to these images, even as metaphors, we are rejecting the real universe:

1. God existed before the universe.
2. God created the universe.
3. God knows everything.
4. God plans what happens.
5. God can choose to violate the laws of nature.

I know that approaching with any level of scientific rigor something so personal, so cherished, so core touching as God may be hard at first. But the price of a real God is that we have to consciously let go of what makes it unreal. God can't be everything or it will be nothing. We all need hope and comfort and inspiration, but we also need the built-in bullshit detector of science.

If you've never taken these five ideas literally but instead have seen God as simply a word for the sense of wonder, of the unknown, of endless possibility, of cosmic connection, and of the opportunity to not need all the answers, then it may perhaps seem silly to bother refuting them one by one. Yet I would be surprised if your sense of wonder, of the unknown cosmic connection, and endless possibility connected with the idea of God was not based on an unconscious lifelong association of God with at least some of these impossible characteristics.

1. God could not have existed before the universe.

The history of the universe tells us that *complexity evolves* from simpler states of being, so there could not have been an intelligence complex enough to design anything at all, let alone a universe, before cosmic evolution even began.

What I'm about to say about the universe is based not only on direct astronomical observations but also on supercomputer simulations. The two standard ways of doing astronomy used to be theory and observation, but simulation is a new way. Direct observation of the universe in many cases is impossible, since dark matter and dark energy, which are most of the universe, are invisible, and because events on the scale of the universe happen across such vast stretches of time that a human lifetime is far too short to experience them. Theory is also inadequate because, no matter how sophisticated it may be, it can't predict in any detail the kind of awesome *transformations* that had to happen for primordial particles and energy to turn into galaxies, stars, and planets. But supercomputers can predict them, to a surprising degree. The availability of supercomputers is a key reason why scientific cosmology has entered a golden age.

Supercomputers enable scientists to collapse billions of years of evolution into minutes, and billions of light-years onto a computer screen. My husband's team of astrophysicists, for example, has several times simulated the evolution, from the Big Bang to today, of a representative cube of universe a billion light-years on a side. The team ran the simulations according to different theoretical assumptions in order to test those assumptions. The supercomputer—the equivalent of fourteen thousand top-of-the-line Intel computers working for two months—can track the motions of many billions of particles and cross-correlate their interactions with *all* the others for (a simulated) 13.8 billion years.

My husband's team then compares the final universe produced by the simulation to the real universe as telescopes directly observe it; the computers predict what the observational astronomers will find. Only if the simulated and real universes match were the initial assumptions right. They match in incredible detail.* When the simulation is not stopped at today but allowed to run, we are watching a simulation of the future of our universe.

Not only cosmology but many fields, from neuroscience to climate science, have leaped ahead since the advent of supercomputer simulation. Here, in an abbreviated and simplified form, is what modern cosmology tells us about our origins.

Right after the Big Bang there was nothing but rapidly moving elementary particles and energy, not even atoms yet, though the simplest atoms, hydrogen and helium, formed after a few hundred thousand years. The early universe was smooth, expanding but not turbulent. Spacetime (space and time in the universe have since Einstein been understood to be a continuum) came into existence wrinkled, and the wrinkles expanded with the universe. For billions of years primeval particles of dark matter flowed toward the wrinkles by gravitational attraction alone. The dark matter formed clumps along the wrinkles through a process that astronomers enigmatically call "violent relaxation." Up to here, our cosmic history was simple, governed by pure physics. Scientists deeply understand that era. But as time passed, enormous transformations came about, and the complexity that resulted is much harder to understand. The immense gravity of the dark matter clumps drew in clouds of hydrogen and helium, which cooled and collapsed to the centers of the clumps, igniting as stars. Surrounded by a halo of dark matter, the stars cooked up inside themselves the heavier atoms, like oxygen, carbon, nitrogen, silicon, and the nearly a hundred natural

*You can watch visualizations of these simulations on the website for the most recent book I coauthored with my husband, *The New Universe and the Human Future*, http://new -universe.org.

atoms that are heavier than helium and make up most of the periodic table of the elements. The biggest stars exploded in supernovas and spewed these heavy atoms into space as pure stardust to soar for eons. The intermingling stardust of thousands of supernovas, which had occurred over many eras, got pulled into the gravitational field of our forming solar system, and 4.6 billion years ago the stardust condensed into the rocky planets, including Earth. Hundreds of millions of years passed before the earliest life evolved here, and billions more before intelligence evolved that was complex enough to understand the idea of creation. The evolution of such complexity takes a long time.

This is the kind of universe we live in. This is where our thinking should start.

Something as complex as a mind capable of planning and creating the universe could not possibly have been there to do so.

What's more, it's not clear where "there" would be, since cosmologists are continually pushing back the beginning. The Big Bang used to be thought of as the beginning, but the larger theory of cosmic inflation now explains what set up the initial conditions for the Big Bang and caused the wrinkles that later attracted dark matter. The theory of cosmic inflation has made five specific predictions, and the four that have been tested so far have all been confirmed by observation, so the theory has become part of the standard model of cosmology. Astrophysicists have also extrapolated backward from cosmic inflation, theorizing what may have happened before. This theory is called *eternal inflation*, and it posits a pure quantum state of being outside our universe that, once begun, can never stop and may continue eternally, producing multiple universes, including ours. Where, in that case, would the beginning be?

Let's suppose the theory of eternal inflation turns out to be right. Does eternal into the future require eternal into the past? Not clear. It's not even clear what "eternal into the past" might mean. In eternal inflation not even an atom can form. No information can be preserved in any way, and thus no meaningful past could exist.

Furthermore, "eternal into the future" is not even a meaningful concept *inside* our universe. The largest structures in our universe are called superclusters of galaxies. They will exist for many billions more years, but gradually the dark energy that's causing the universe to expand faster and faster will tear them apart. Unlike superclusters of galaxies, our own galaxy, the Milky Way, is bound together by gravity, which will permanently prevent dark energy from tearing it apart. Instead our Milky Way will merge in five billion years or so with our neighboring large galaxy, Andromeda, and tens of smaller nearby galaxies will also fall into the forming megagalaxy that we might call Milky Andromeda. New stars will keep forming, and Milky Andromeda will shine on for a *trillion* more years, hundreds of times longer than Earth has existed. That's pretty close to eternal—but not the same.

The fact is, "in the beginning" is no more precise than "once upon a time." The beginning is just a line we draw in our minds to be able to start telling a story. The end is a line we draw to stop. They have no objective reality. They can't even be defined, let alone explained. So demanding to know the very beginning of the universe is as misguided as trying to understand the last moment of the universe.

2. *God could not have created the universe.*
The universe evolved, and once life got a foothold on Earth, life evolved. If God did exist before the universe, could He have created the universe by setting evolution off and *using evolution as His means of creation?* That theory doesn't work. Evolution is not a path that can be used to achieve anything intentional. Biological evolution is unpredictable in principle because it depends on random mutations interacting with a changing environment. So if a Creator God had any particular intention before starting—for example, to create a creature like us—that would never be what ended up evolving.

We've all heard the charge that "evolution is unproved because it's only a theory." But this misunderstands the whole nature of science. Evolution is the foundational theory of all biology, and almost

all progress in medicine, agriculture, and ecology for the last century and a half has been based on it. The critics refuse to accept
the theory unless it's proved beyond question (although they're usu-
ally happy to accept medicine if they're sick). But a scientific theory
can never be proved beyond question or it would not be scientific.
Mathematical theorems can be proved but not theories about the
natural world. A scientific theory always remains open to further investigation, and a future discovery could rule it out. If a theory can't
be ruled out *no matter what data surface*, it's not science. It's dogma.

Many atheists have used the impossibility of God's creating the
universe to argue that therefore God does not exist, case closed.
But in fact this doesn't rule out God. It only rules out a God that
existed before the universe and created it. Why does God have to
have created the universe? Millions of people have prayed to gods
who didn't create the universe. Surely that is not essential for a God
to be real, inspiring, and helpful. It's not possible anyway.

The nature of the universe can teach us about God and free us
from the fuzzy thinking that is preventing us from demanding—and
discovering—a real God.

3. God can't know everything.

To require that God be or have a mind, however omniscient and
perfect, is to embalm God like a mummy in the tight wrappings of
our own self-image. God has no cosmic mind that can *know* things
the way we use that word. In our universe there is simply no unified
view of the whole. This is one of the many weird implications of
Einstein's theory of relativity, and there's no way to get around it.

There are three strikes against the possibility of omniscience.
Knowledge requires information, and the speed of light sets a top
limit on how fast any information can travel: 186,000 miles per
second (300,000 km/sec). But space itself can expand at any speed,
without limit. All the distant galaxies are receding from our galaxy,
and the farther away they are, the faster they're receding, until at
a certain distance they are receding faster than the speed of light.

(What's actually happening is that the space between us and them is expanding faster than the speed of light, not that the galaxies are moving faster than the speed of light.) At that distance galaxies disappear from our visible universe, because their light (and the light from any galaxies beyond them) cannot cross space that is expanding faster than the speed of light. Their light will thus never reach us, creating a cosmic horizon. Yet we have every reason to expect that those galaxies can see their neighbors, though not us, and that evolution is proceeding there, as it does here. But no one can know directly. Not even God.

What we call the visible universe is only a small patch of the larger universe created by the Big Bang. It's visible to us because light has had time to get to us from its farthest reaches. But from the viewpoint of any particular location, there hasn't been time enough since the Big Bang for light or information to have arrived from the rest of the expanding universe outside the visible patch. No matter where you are, you're surrounded by a horizon. The universe beyond your visible patch is a kind of "elsewhen" that is simply over the rainbow. No unified intelligence or perception could ever know the details of what was going on or had gone on *everywhere*.

Here's the second strike against omniscience: events occurring at different locations don't happen in a certain order. If two spaceships are moving at a significant fraction of the speed of light with respect to each other, they will see events happen in different orders. It's not their perception; things really do happen in a different order when viewed from different frames of reference, because time is not the smooth and regular clockwork that common sense assumes. What is past depends on where you are and how fast you're moving with respect to other observers. There *is* no overall truth for God to know. Most truth is local.

And strike three: light from distant galaxies is stretched as it crosses expanding space before it arrives at our telescopes. Although its *speed* on arrival is unchanged, its *wavelength* (which determines its color) expands just as much as the universe has expanded since the light was emitted. The stretching wavelength causes colors to become redder. This "redshift" is precisely measurable and tells us how much the universe has expanded since the light left each galaxy. By plugging this information into the double dark theory, astronomers can know how far away that galaxy was when it emitted the light and how far away it is now. All space is filled with redshift information moving every which way, readable by intelligent beings on any world. The universe is not only the way it looks today to us but is also all the ways it looks to other worlds, based on the information reaching viewers there from different places at different times. Galaxies are forming and colliding, and all their stars and planets are moving. The sky is a collage that is different for every viewer in the cosmos.

The natural temptation is to get around these limits to omniscience by claiming that God is "everywhere" and thus knows all local knowledge and sees all viewpoints, but the cosmic speed limit would prevent such a God from even being aware of its own full self. Could we say that God *is* the universe? We could say it, but how would that help? We already have a name for the universe. A synonym would add nothing so valuable to our lives or understanding that it could outweigh the suffering and conflict that attachments to God have cost, and continue to cost, humanity. God has to be hugely valuable to compensate for that.

"Everything is God" was a daring and philosophically explosive idea when Spinoza put it forth in the seventeenth century. It was also Einstein's view. "I believe in Spinoza's God who reveals himself in the harmony of all that exists," Einstein wrote, "but not in a God who concerns himself with the fate and actions of human beings."

I feel drawn to those who see God as the source and substance of all reality, because it can be such a life-affirming attitude and reflect a beautiful sense of wonder and gratitude. But at bottom this idea of God is only a perspective on what we already know. It's not the discovery of a God that could be real. A God that is the source and substance of reality would have had to exist before and outside the universe. There is no way we could contact such a God and no way such a God could contact us, and this is why Einstein added that his God is unconcerned with the fate and actions of human beings. I think with today's knowledge we can do better.

4. God doesn't plan what happens.

It's not hard to feel anger at God when someone you love and desperately prayed for suffers or dies. Or when you miss the opportunity of a lifetime by a hair. I confess I sometimes felt angry at a God I didn't even believe existed. It was as though I instinctively expected some kind of cosmic justice. But expecting cosmic justice will drive me to distraction, because it requires that I assign blame, and blaming can become an obsession. Why doesn't God answer my prayers? Why is my life not as good as so-and-so's? The fact is, whatever the reason may be, *God had nothing to do with it.* Since God has no unified will or mind, there's none there to make and evaluate a plan.

If a plan existed, what would that even mean? A plan at its most basic level is an image or intention that exists *today* of something that might exist *at some point* in the future. Not the entire future.

Planning the future of the universe is impossible. Whizzing elementary particles make up our bodies, our brains, and our world. Even though statistically the collective behavior of elementary particles can be predicted to a ridiculous number of decimal places, the behavior of any single particle cannot be predicted *in principle*, according to quantum physics. But what a single particle does can matter. One random cosmic ray hitting a replicating DNA molecule can send evolution off in a new direction. There is no way a mind, as we use the word, could keep track of individual particles, let alone predict and control them. No plan could exist, not today and not 13.8 billion years ago, that could foretell, let alone control, the infinite future motions of every elementary particle, including those that don't exist yet.

Randomness plays a big role in our lives. Sometimes things happen to us for no reason other than we were there, and lives can be shaped or shattered that way. The future of any given person is unpredictable because it's subject to countless interacting possibilities, each of which in turn is subject to countless interacting possibilities, ad infinitum. And yet surprisingly, just as with elementary particles, statistical probabilities can be determined. The number of people who will be killed on US highways next Labor Day weekend or shot in Chicago next year can be predicted with eerie accuracy, but the identities of those people cannot. There is no plan for any individual. God could never predict or control what any one of us does.

But what about the nonhuman world? The animal kingdom is complex and interrelated and beautiful. How could it ever have come about by chance? Chance or God are not the real alternatives here. Evolution is not the same as chance. Chance is the flip of a coin, but biological evolution is countless intricate experiments, each result tested as rigorously as anything can be by this world and living on only if it keeps passing every test. No living creature evolved by chance. Every single one is the descendant of countless generations of survivors.

The sun, moon, and stars didn't come about by chance. They came about because matter and energy follow the laws of physics, and laws are the opposite of chance. Even chance follows statistical laws. This is an orderly universe—or so we understand it.

Could God be the laws of physics? Laws don't plan. They have no mind or judgment. Calling the laws of physics God is not useful, either to physics or anything else, and we already have a name for the laws of physics.

The hallmark of human intelligence is the ability to look at complexity and see design in it. Design is not inherent in the world out there. Design is what our brains construct. When our eyes watch a sunset glowing over the ocean, our brains don't take in a complete scene like a movie. Instead light flows into our eyes, and one part of the nervous system detects horizontal and vertical lines, another detects color, another movement, and so on, and the brain pieces them together to construct a meaningful picture. Intelligence abstracts a design out of nature with metaphors and reasoning and strives to express it and share it.

What we're really talking about is pattern. Every child has the ability to discern patterns—in clouds, for example. Almost every culture discerned patterns in the stars and named a set of constellations. Finding patterns is the way intelligent beings create order from chaos, so that we can see the same reality as each other. This helps us to be able to cooperate.

For those who believe in God's plan, the painful part is accepting all its contents. There will always be unexpected bad things happening, as well as some good things. It's easy to ascribe the good things that happen to God, but what about the bad? Can we comfort ourselves with the theory that what appear to be bad things are not really bad but serve some larger purpose? This is a theory that can never be disproved, no matter how much it may harm us and no matter what conflicting data may surface. What if the theory is wrong? How will we ever know? The belief that God plans everything puts the blame for random misfortunes, for which no one is to blame, either on God, leading to anger and resentment, or on ourselves for not trusting God enough. What it doesn't do is help us deal productively with the real world by understanding probabilities and accepting and working with the nature of the universe that we actually live in. We are the ones who must plan.

5. *God cannot violate the laws of nature.*
Nothing that exists in the real universe can violate the laws of nature, since what exists is an expression of those laws. If something real looks like a violation, it's because we haven't fully understood the laws. Anything real is real because it is permitted by nature and in harmony with it. The belief that God can violate the laws

of nature is based on something much deeper than logic: it's based on the assumption that the spiritual realm where God presides is somehow separate from and independent of the physical universe, so that *God is unconstrained by the laws of physics*. In other words, God can do anything He wants, because He exists in a realm where the known laws don't apply. This nonphysical God is assumed to be able to reach from that realm into the universe of laws to affect events in our world. Valiant attempts to explain how God could do this have kept theologians busy for centuries. The idea that God is unconstrained by the laws governing the physical world may have been reasonable in the Middle Ages, when God's realm was believed to surround the universe of the heavenly spheres. It might have made sense in an era before people understood the modern meaning of *physical*. But those times are past. A new picture of the universe has given us a new understanding of the meaning of physical.

It turns out, perhaps shockingly, that most of the *physical* universe is *spiritual to us* in the sense that the only way we can ever relate to it is spiritually. Modern cosmology has changed forever the fascinating relationship between the spiritual and the physical—a change I'll explore in detail in chapter 4.

This list of what God can't be generally agrees with most atheists' reasons for concluding that therefore God does not exist. But this is no place to stop. We've merely stated what God can't be. We haven't considered yet what God *could* be.

MODERN ALTERNATIVES

During the many years I spent searching for some coherent way to think about God, I came across several alternatives that scientifically responsible people, with the best of intentions, had proposed as consistent with science. Here are some of them: "God is the process of evolution"; "God is the endless creativity of the universe"; "God is the process of radical transformation"; "God is a personification of the universe." Like the "everything is God" perspective, there is something wonderful about these outlooks. They reframe reality itself, whatever it may be, as sacred and our very existence here as miraculous. They are honest, conceptually grand, and highly respectful of believers. I hope they inspire many people to enlarge their thinking. If my life ran well and I had no need for anything but gratitude, these views of God would deepen my spirituality far more than the discounted views I discussed earlier. But the problem for me is that I'm an addict, and my life doesn't run well on its own. I actually *need* a higher power.

So the problem for me is that nothing can be asked of such gods. Evolution is impersonal and pitiless. Creativity and transformation, wondrous and crucial though they are, are equally impersonal. Calling the universe itself God doesn't really add anything to our understanding of God but diminishes the universe by wrapping such a human-shaped image around it.

One feature that unites these alternatives is that they allow people to hold on to the idea that God somehow created the universe and is bigger and more fundamental than the universe. If God is the process of evolution, then God was there in the beginning and has led to everything, even if He had no plan. If God is endless creativity or radical transformation or the universe itself—or all of them—God was there in the beginning and created everything. But preserving the impossible option that God was there in the beginning is going to hold us back from discovering a genuine and thrilling possibility of this universe.

If God is not to be lost in euphemisms or vagueness but is to be of service to those of us who need it, it must be *something*, something unique. The challenge is to identify *what* it might be, among the myriad possibilities of this brave new universe. This requires limiting God—it can't be everything—but limiting God in no way belittles God.

In fact, it opens radically new directions.

The scientific revolution of today is bringing us closer than ever to the possibility of a coherent and meaningful big picture in which we can bring our full selves—our emotions, our growing scientific and historical knowledge, our spiritual values, our origin story, and our sense of place in the universe—into harmony. To succeed we need a way to think about God that supports, rather than thwarts, this harmony. We're ready for a God that could be real.

CHAPTER 3

A God That Could Be Real

Science can be brutal in placing truth above human consequences, although that's also why it's trustworthy. At the end of chapter 2, it seemed that science supported atheists' arguments against God. Many old assumptions about God, once exposed to the light, are revealed as unreliable. So we begin again, this time with nothing—perhaps feeling humbled, perhaps even distraught. This must be the way the Europeans of the 1600s felt when Galileo proved that their entire picture of the cosmos could not be right. Suddenly the heavenly spheres and their music disappeared, and people faced infinite emptiness with no place for God. But that bleak vision isn't necessary. Science allows us to see the God that *can't* be real, but it also allows us to discover a God that *can* be real, if we choose to.

Until very recent times people didn't get to choose their own God. In most places they still don't. The invitation in the twelve-step programs to turn to *God as you understand God* is in itself a revelation to millions of newcomers. Do you mean I get to design my own God? they ask, incredulous. Not only do you get to—you must. Because whatever image of God you were using before, if any, has not worked for you, or you wouldn't be in a program like this. I needed God to arise from the principles that govern reality. One of these principles, which is not yet widely known, turns out to be the key. It's called emergence, and it's a central idea of modern science—and absolutely central to understanding a God that could be real.

Emergence is the source of most of the creativity of this universe. At its simplest it works like this: When the complexity of any inter- acting system increases enough, the system turns into something completely new. The individual parts remain what they are, but seen together they merge, and something radically original *emerges*, and it follows new laws. As the physicist Phil Anderson summed it up, "More is different."

Here's a simple example: The air molecules in the room you're sitting in now are flying about at something like a thousand miles per hour, constantly bumping into each other, your clothes and skin, and the furniture and walls of the room. A vast cacophony of in- teractions is going on among the molecules, but out of that arise temperature and pressure. Temperature and pressure are scientifi- cally real phenomena; they can be precisely measured, and there are known relations between them. But individual molecules have no temperature or pressure. The laws that govern temperature and pressure are among the laws of physics, but those laws don't apply to *anything* until enough molecules have gathered together. Where did those laws come from? It turns out that they emerge from the collective behavior of myriad particles.

Emergence may sound like magic, but in fact it was a discovery.

By the 1850s physicists in England, France, and Germany had created the new field of thermodynamics, which explained tempera- ture, heat, and pressure and made it possible to build much more ef- ficient engines of all kinds, as well as better transportation, heating, and cooling systems. Thermodynamics was hugely powerful tech- nologically, but no one understood why it worked. The new field postulated two laws about closed systems:

First law of thermodynamics: Energy is neither gained nor lost.

Second law of thermodynamics: Entropy never decreases.

Entropy was a word invented by the German physicist Rudolf Clausius. He intended it to sound a little like *energy* but with *trop* in it, from the Greek for "transformation," because entropy has to do with one-way change. Perfume will evaporate from a tiny open bottle into the whole room but will never spontaneously come together again in the bottle. An ice cube in your drink will melt but never refreeze to re-form even the smallest piece of the ice cube, even though it would cost no extra energy to do so and would therefore be perfectly consistent with the first law. But perfume never returns to the bottle and the water never refreezes because that would violate the second law. What was the underlying explanation for the mysterious second law?

At the time many physicists resisted the atomic theory because there was no physical evidence for atoms. Despite that, in the 1870s the Austrian physicist Ludwig Boltzmann, daring to take atoms as real, explained how *entropy emerges statistically* from the combined randomness of zillions of atoms. Entropy, he realized, is a measurement of disorder. Once an ordered deck of cards is shuffled, it is exceedingly unlikely that further random shuffling will restore the original order. Once we are dealing with not just fifty-two cards but instead zillions of atoms, randomness rules. Complex systems can never spontaneously become less disordered.

Boltzmann was able to give the first precise explanation of how a higher-level phenomenon like entropy emerges. He succeeded, however, only because he was dealing with pure physics, and there was no spark of life involved to outwit expectations. But when emergence happens in living creatures—the simplest of which is vastly more complicated than a box of atoms—a new factor comes into play. Living things collectively can create "self-organizing systems." How does a self-organizing system emerge? An anthill is an example.

Ants are fabulously successful from an evolutionary point of view, as Steven Johnson explains in his lively book, *Emergence*. They're on every continent except, ironically, Antarctica. Collectively they bulldoze immense amounts of the surface of the earth, redistributing nutrients. But no ant knows this. They communicate by (involuntarily) emitting and responding to pheromones (scent molecules). According to the biologist E. O. Wilson, 90 percent of the communications of some ants are chemical and only 10 percent occur by direct contact. Apparently they don't rely much on their eyes. They can recognize a dozen or so pheromones and sense where those pheromones are more intense. They also recognize the frequency with which they encounter other ants and can note the difference between meeting two ants and two hundred ants in a minute. That's about the extent of their individual communication abilities. But if we observe ten thousand of them in a colony, we realize that a "swarm logic" has emerged. A harvest ant *colony* is continually adjusting the number of ants foraging for food, based on several factors: the number of mouths to feed, how much food is stored in the nest, how much food is available in the vicinity, and whether other colonies are out there competing. The colony prioritizes food sources based on distance and accessibility. Yet no ant understands any of this. The colony can engineer the construction of an anthill taller than a man. Over many years the colony will go through predictable stages of development, from daring youth to conservative maturity to death, yet each ant lives only a tiny fraction of that time. What is going on? How does swarm logic emerge?

Each ant simply pays attention to its nearest neighbors and to pheromone trails. It doesn't wait for orders. It doesn't know how many foragers or trash collectors are on duty at any given time, but it can keep track of how many of each worker it has run into in its daily movements, because different jobs are associated with different pheromones, and these make the ant adjust its own behavior. Based on a few simple rules, the social system is self-organizing in a way that is astonishingly successful. Ants don't have free choice. They follow the local rules. To solve the kind of problems we would hand over to experts, the colony uses statistical probabilities. For every ant that overestimates a number, there'll be one that underestimates and the result is a wash. The colony is a higher-level organism that has far more sophisticated abilities than its members do. *Or so we humans understand it.*

The emergent behavior of a colony of social insects is a discovery by human beings. What the colony is doing on the large scale is something a *consciousness* must be sufficiently large scale to perceive and give meaning to. We humans are able to do this because our kind of intelligence discerns abstract patterns in social behavior and constructs theories.

The endless creativity of emergence has underlain all of evolution. About a billion and a half years ago simple microorganisms came together and formed the first eukaryotic cells, the kind of cells our bodies are made of. That was emergence. Each cell is like a little city, peopled with a nucleus and interconnected organelles, some of which continue to reproduce themselves inside the cell with their own DNA. About half a billion years ago those early cells began to specialize, creating the first creatures with distinct organs. That too was emergence.

As animal bodies evolved and became more complex, their brains had to evolve to be able to run the bodies and coordinate all the complicated interactions with their environments. As brains evolved in competence and complexity, consciousness emerged, and even self-consciousness in us and a few other creatures like elephants, dolphins, whales, and several primates and smart birds. Each of those momentous steps in evolution saw the emergence of entirely new phenomena, without which you and I would never have come into existence. Not every step of evolution is an emergent phenomenon; emergence refers to the great *qualitative* differences that occur only rarely.

Emergence is still a relatively new field, and there are schools of thought that sometimes conflict. A number of scientists are working to generate a rigorous set of criteria for the physical, chemical, and biological bases for emergent phenomena, but according to Ursula Goodenough, the biologist, emergence theorist, and author of the trail-blazing book *The Sacred Depths of Nature*, the core understandings about emergence go something like this:

1. Molecules have shapes. Water, for example, is V-shaped, its large oxygen atom at the vertex and its two hydrogen atoms extending outward, with the oxygen carrying a net negative charge and the hydrogens a net positive charge. Put many water molecules together in a container at room temperature, and, although they are all zooming around, they have picosecond interactions with one another, positive to negative. The result is that they form a liquid that has properties, like viscosity and surface tension. Viscosity is not a property of a single water molecule; it is the emergent property of countless water-water relationships. Put this container in the freezer and the molecules stop moving around and the positive-to-negative relationships stabilize, so ice has different emergent properties, like hardness. The emergent properties arise because of relationships between components.

2. The biochemistry that occurs in living organisms works in much the same way, except the molecules are larger; the most important are proteins. Proteins, which are encoded by genes, fold into shapes that facilitate their interactions with one another and with other molecules in the cell. These interactions generate emergent properties, like metabolism and cell division. Again, metabolism is not a property of a single protein molecule—it pops through as the result of many molecular interactions.

3. The emergent properties of an organism are called its traits. If we were to list the traits of a worm, for example, we might include its motility (wiggly) and its texture (slimy). A gene mutation often results in a mutant protein with a different shape, which can alter the nature of its interactions with other proteins in the organism. A mutant protein in the slime-generation pathway might give rise to a worm that is slimier than other

worms. If this allows the worm to move more readily through the soil to obtain food, then worms carrying the mutant gene are more likely to be found in future generations; conversely, if it causes soil particles to stick to the worm and slow it down, then the mutant gene is not likely to spread into the population. The key point here is that natural selection, the driver of biological evolution, acts on traits—that is, it acts on emergent properties. Natural selection doesn't "see" genes or proteins; it sees only the consequences of protein interactions.

4. A key property of traits is that they are *about* something, *for* something. Vision, the emergent property of numerous protein pathways in the eye and the brain, can be said to have a *purpose* or *goal*. The individual proteins, and the individual eye and brains cells that harbor them, lack this purpose. *The goal-oriented features arise through emergence.*

As Goodenough sums up the idea of emergence, "Something else emerges from nothing but."

In our own lives we can perceive the emergence of new realities at repeatedly higher levels of complexity—but it takes a theory of emergence. Once we perceive a higher, emergent level, we have to make an effort to discover the laws that govern it. By definition they're not implicit in the laws governing the lower levels (although they must be consistent with those laws). As a result, outside of a few fields like thermodynamics no one can fully understand how an emergent phenomenon works by reasoning from how its constituent parts work. There is no way to understand ant society by studying a few ants.

The study of individual organisms and social insects—as well as the study of economics, political science, social psychology, ecology, evolutionary biology, and many other fields—are all attempts to understand phenomena that have emerged from different kinds of living, interacting systems. These fields have given us much of our modern understanding of the world. But only in recent years have we begun to grasp that what they all have in common is emergence. The essence of emergence is unpredicted newness, and naming and studying that newness keeps expanding our perspective on reality.

EMERGENT PHENOMENA ARE REAL

An emergent phenomenon is not just an organizing tool: it is truly a new *entity*. This cannot be emphasized enough. The emergent phenomenon is something radically new, different from its constituent parts. It triggers, if not creates, new laws to describe it. Emergent phenomena need to be seen as *just as real* as their constituent parts—which are often emergent phenomena themselves. Emergent systems persist over time, outlasting any of their component parts.

In this way large organizations and endeavors emerge from aspects of human behavior, and they are real *but not human*. They don't behave anything like a human being. They can be in many places at once but never in jail. They feel no joy or pain. They have no beliefs and no compassion, even if almost all the individual humans whose work feeds into them do.

What, for example, is a market? When large numbers of people are trading goods, services, or information for money, the market determines the price of those things at any given time. There's a market in corn, in oil, in stocks, in everything people want and trade. Millions of people make decisions about where to spend or invest varying amounts of money. Markets even affect the value of the money. No one, including the professionals, understands all the rules; no one can predict outcomes every time, though many try; and a constantly varying cast of characters is participating and influencing every market. What a market is, is impossible to pin down. There are competing economic theories. Just as temperature doesn't exist for a couple of molecules, a market doesn't exist if there are only a couple of participants. Nevertheless markets do *exist*. They speak with precision, and we grant them immense power. They affect the price and availability of everything we buy. A market is a higher level of complexity than any of its participants can fully understand; it emerges from the interacting collective economic ambitions, reasoning, actions, opportunities, resources, and opinions of a vast number of people. It's an emergent phenomenon. "The market" can seem to have its own intelligence. Once "the market has spoken," there is no appeal to a higher authority. Millions defer to its wisdom.

When we think of all the markets interacting together, something new and far more difficult to comprehend emerges—the global economy. Here not only do economists fail to understand the key rules—they don't even know what factors the rules should govern. But no one denies that the global economy is real.

Similarly it's hard to deny that the media, though grammatically plural, is singular in its cumulative impact. It's a pervasive shaper of our society. The media is the mutually reinforcing impact of the Internet, television, publications, radio, movies, and so on, which together create celebrity, manipulate political tides, influence ideas and aesthetics, and energetically sculpt our culture. To the great media theorist Marshall McLuhan, the media was even broader, including everything made by humans that influences the way people think; for example, the clothing a person wears communicates something about her, and that communication, regardless of what it actually may say, is part of McLuhan's media. People may quibble about the definition of *media*, but no one questions that it exists.

The media has the power not only to shape public opinion through selection of stories, frame, perspective, and frequency of repetition; it can shape our emotions, our desires, put great numbers of us into fear or excitement, or make us hate or worship someone or something. Whatever sense of our historical moment that people today don't get from their own expertise, they get from the media or from friends and personal contacts who are affected by the media. The media's influence penetrates the most intimate goings-on within our private lives, such as what we should eat, what diagnosis explains our child's behavior, or what we should expect from a spouse. Countless billions of dollars are spent around the world on the premise that no power is more real than the power of the media.

But what is the media? There's no there there. The media, as a whole, can't be pointed to. It's not even a legal fiction. It's an emergent phenomenon.

Emergent phenomena like the media and the economy have immense influence on our lives and minds—immeasurably more than does the expansion of the distant universe, which no astronomer doubts is real. Powerful emergent phenomena need to be experienced as *real*. The only alternative is to see them as nothing in themselves—just a lot of individual people doing stuff. But if emergent phenomena are not real, then we have to deny our own existence, because we large animals *are* emergent phenomena. We emerged from clumps of cells, and they emerged from elementary particles, with many levels of emergence in between.

If emergent phenomena are not real, then the only things that can be real are those that did not evolve: photons, quarks, and other elementary particles whizzing aimlessly and meaninglessly. We would be making the insane claim that the evolution of the galaxies, of life, and of consciousness has been nothing more than the movement of particles and is completely describable with quantum mechanics. There are some physicists and philosophers who argue this position, but I have yet to meet one who lives as if he actually believes it. Because to do so would require a decision that we ourselves are an illusion—in whose mind I don't know. It's a self-sabotaging place to start if you're a human being looking for a coherent big picture. If we are not real by our physical standards, then we are insane by our psychological standards. This is not only an unhealthy philosophy—it's not supported by science.

What's real about *me* isn't just the atoms I'm made of—they were in most cases somewhere else just a few weeks or at most a few years ago, while *I* have been living continuously since the middle of the last century. What's that *I*? Whatever it is, it's real by my standards. Because if it isn't, there's nobody here writing this.

If the economy, the media, and, just as important, the government are not considered real, then in bowing to their enormous power we humans are letting imaginary ghosts run our lives. We're not. They're real. They're just not human.

This book is an exploration of what we choose to call real, because this choice is our opportunity. In a modern scientific understanding God can be real.

But if God was not there in the beginning of the universe, how can God be real today? It had to come into existence. But how?

Emergence tells us that as the complexity of a situation grows, we can predict with confidence that something radically original will emerge, governed by never-before-seen laws. But what that something will be, or what new laws may be revealed, cannot be predicted even in principle. The complexity theorist Stuart Kauffman has gone a step further to say that not only can the next stage not be predicted but the possible next stages can't even be given probabilities. They are "radically unpredictable." If he's right, then no one may ever understand the moment of transformation. Yet we can count on it.

When we apply the idea of emergence to the immense complexity of human interactions, it becomes apparent that something astonishing *must* come into being. Something real but utterly godlike.

God is an emergent phenomenon that can have emerged only from humanity.

EMERGED FROM WHERE?

When I was fifteen and the rabbi became furious at me for writing that God was a fiction created by humans, I was right in believing that humans were not created by God, but I then jumped to conclusions, because I didn't think scientifically. I didn't understand that you can't conclude what's true from simply eliminating one false possibility. Here are the two crucial mistakes I made at fifteen: that humans came on the scene before God does not mean humans *created* God, and it doesn't make God a *fiction*.

Humans didn't create God intentionally, the way they created cars. There's a crucial difference between "emergence" as a result of human intentions and emergence in nature. When we look beneath the hood of a car, we see many parts whose interaction generates an emergent property—automotive motility—through many emergent subsystems: ignition, acceleration, cooling, and so on. But a car engine doesn't construct itself; the parts are prefabricated and assembled by humans. In contrast an organism is said to *self-organize*. When a human egg is fertilized and starts to cleave into two and then four and then eight cells and on to a trillion cells in the newborn, different sets of genes are expressed in different cells, and the resulting different sets of proteins interact to generate distinctive embryonic and then fetal and then newborn traits. The mother is not on the observation deck giving orders. The interactions between cells are key to this process: during brain development, for example, protobrain cells (neurons) migrate into the cranium, making physical contacts and secreting hormones that influence the migration and final location of each one, eventually generating minds that are capable of learning, memory, and language. Emergence undergirds every step of this remarkable process. The mother may have no clue how the process works and is in some sense right in feeling, as many mothers do, that what has emerged is not her creation but a miracle.

My second mistake: God is not a fiction. Our ancestors over tens of thousands of years *collectively* gave rise to almost everything that is now most important to us and most influential in our lives. Cooking, language, agriculture, technologies, government, the economy, science, education, art, religion—are these fictions? They're abstractions that emerged from different aspects of human behavior, and they're real, even though no one can completely define what any one of them actually is.

God has emerged from some aspect of us, something we were already doing in prehistory, something so ancient and fundamental that it was in our ancestors before the first ideas of gods arose. It has to be so basic to us that without it, we might not be human. What could that be?

What truly defines us?

Since ancient Greece, philosophers and later scientists have struggled with the definition of *human*. Some have defined us by our intelligence, others by our ability to make tools, and still others by our facility with language. But recent findings don't support those theories. We're not the only toolmakers; many primates use sticks or grass to fish termites out of logs and stones to crack nuts. We're not the only thinkers; a species of crow has been shown to reason out simple mechanical problems in advance without even having to go through trial and error. We're not the only communicators; many animals communicate warnings, invitations, pleasure, and threats by sounds and signals. So what makes us distinctive?

We have no evidence that other animals use their abilities to create meaning or a better life for their children than they had. When you really come down to it, what makes us distinctive is that we humans change and grow not just because we have to in order to adapt to external conditions *but because we aspire to something more*. Intelligence, toolmaking, and language help make us human, but they would never have developed as they did if our ancestors had not been aspiring to do something better than it had been done before.

Aspirations are not the same as desires, like food, sex, and security. Every animal has these desires from instinct alone. Aspirations reach beyond survival needs, to something that *shapes* each of us into an individual. Aspiration isn't always to create; it could be to restrain ourselves to fit in better. We all aspire to different things.

We humans are the aspiring species.

Because we feel driven to be better, to do better, to create better, to understand better, to have more, to be safer, we have become far more than the sum of our instincts. The interacting aspirations of humanity make up an extremely complex system, and this is true even in isolated communities. From the expanding complexity of generations of aspirations mixing and cross-fertilizing, gods emerged virtually everywhere there were people.

As we pull back the zoom lens on reality, expanding our frame of reference by orders of magnitude, the world and universe become new, beyond not only prediction but previous imagination.

God is endlessly emerging from the staggering complexity of all humanity's aspirations across time.

GOD EMERGES FROM HUMANITY'S ASPIRATIONS

Are aspirations real enough that they can conglomerate and result in an emergent phenomenon? If we ourselves are real—and we've already established that—then our aspirations must be real, because they are our defining characteristics; they are our purpose. They play out in our behavior and beliefs and interactions with each other. They're affected by what we see other people do, which is largely a playing out of their own aspirations. The aspirations, fulfilled and unfulfilled, of countless people, living and dead, influence our sense of what is possible and desirable and meaningful. To question the reality of our aspirations is to allow the possibility that we are nothing but meat with habits. We know that's not true about ourselves; surely we can't believe that about other people.

Aspirations are the stories of our future, the stories we live for. Aspirations are among the abstractions, like love, that are the most real to us.

The idea that God is a phenomenon that emerges from human aspirations turns out to be astonishingly fertile. It casts human progress in a new light. This ever-emerging God can be understood as the dynamic presence of what humanity has *collectively* achieved. In this sense God is indeed a creator—of toolmaking, ritual, and language and later of ideals like truth, freedom, and equality, which have taken hundreds of generations to clarify in practice.

The emerging God also can be seen as the guiding force of science. If every astronomer, for example, had to start over observing the stars, no one would ever understand anything. Thousands of years of humans aspiring to understand the heavens better, and aspiring to build on each other's work, were necessary to arrive at the science we have today. It's the emerging God that allows us to stand, as Isaac Newton phrased it, on the shoulders of giants. This God has shaped the development of the scientific method from a weaving of many humans' curiosity, rationality, dedication, bravery, and patience. The emerging God has developed meaningful concepts of love and beauty, as well as power and greed. This God is filled with the sense of purpose—not always good purpose but on balance good enough so that we have thrived as a species. Emerging from the collective aspirations, good and bad, that have defined every individual throughout all history and prehistory, God is behind our *shared* drive to control, change, or experience more deeply our lives and our world.

This emergent phenomenon is worthy of the name God. And it may be the only thing that exists in the modern universe that is.

This is not a God that demands worship. Worship is the wrong word, because it implies distance and hierarchy. The emerging God is wherever humans are, and its very existence celebrates our amazing place in the cosmos. *Each of us is directly connected to the emerging God.* We can draw on God's power by identifying with the ancient and uplifting force of aspiration that is in us as members of the human species. No worshipping is necessary.

WHAT IS THE RELATIONSHIP BETWEEN
THE UNIVERSE AND THE EMERGING GOD?

God did not create the universe. *God created the meaning of the universe.* There is something out there that is 13.8 billion years old, from which our galaxy and our solar system evolved, but God had nothing to do with it because God didn't exist then. However, if God had not emerged later, whatever is out there would remain unknown and meaningless, as it is to the other animals on Earth. It wouldn't even be a universe, because "universe" is an idea and there would be no ideas. Only through generations of humans who aspired to share wonder did the emerging God create the concept of "creating the universe." In this sense God has indeed created order from chaos.

God *literally* brings meaning into our lives—not just spiritual meaning, not just purpose, but meaning itself. I see a thing moving, making noise. It's simply there, but God is what makes it a bird walking along the railing of the deck, makes it cute, makes its chirp lovely, makes me want to watch and protect it, rather than eat it, makes me grateful for it and also want to categorize and understand it and its entire genus. Thanks to this emergent process I'm calling God we have concepts, stories, identity, language. They have all emerged from the mixing and catalyzing aspirations of billions of humans over millennia. The emerging God has created the meaning of everything and deepens it moment to moment. The emerging God is where we get our ability to recognize and wonder about the beauty in nature—to find it so exquisite that some people think only a God could have created it. A God did create the most important aspect of it: what it *means to us*. What we do not owe to God we cannot even articulate, because it's meaningless. Without the emerging God, we could not even be grateful for our own biology or existence, because no animal on its own could ever come up with a profound concept like "gratitude" or "biology" or "existence."

This is not just a language game. This is about recognizing the enormity of the aspirational potential of our species and its achievements so far. The emerging God is the source of humanity's insatiable desire for new beauty and wonder, for participation and appreciation, and for stories illuminating where it all came from and how we fit in. The nonstop, long-term, back-and-forth process between every individual and the ever-emerging God of our species has over time constructed a meaningful world so complex that many believe it was handed down by a Creator God—just as the Great

Pyramid of Giza, built by a pharaoh and his workers around 2500 BCE, was believed by the still-ancient Egyptians of 1500 BCE to have been built by an earlier race of godlike beings.

So long as we hold to the belief that God created the universe, we condemn ourselves to live in a tiny imaginary universe, banishing God to a distant place outside it. With this level of denial we will never be able to benefit from the large-scale discoveries of science—or figure out how to live together for the long term here on this very real planet, which is integrated into the very real universe and undergoing very real changes that are challenging us right now to expand our aspirations beyond our personal and local goals.

The old Creator God and the universe that actually surrounds us are incompatible, and trying to reconcile them causes both internal and external strife. To redefine God as an emergent phenomenon, however, may at first feel worse than a little incompatibility. But if you're seeking a big picture that brings into harmony our understanding of God, our growing scientific knowledge, our human emotions, and our fundamental story of ourselves, this is it. Your resistance is God at work, as your aspirations struggle to live in this world.

GOD IS PLANETARY

The emerging God is not universal. It's *planetary*—a phenomenon of Earth. It is humanity's God. The idea that God could be planetary rather than cosmic may sound like a pretty major demotion. But what if it's true?

Do you associate God with hugeness—creating and controlling the *whole* universe, being here *eternally*, before the beginning of time? Many of us have been taught, based on no evidence whatsoever, that God is all or nothing. But what does *all* mean? Even our universe may not be all—no scientist yet knows what *all* includes. What we know is that over time we humans keep learning and creating new ideas. A creative person may produce a new idea every day, but you can't get her future ideas out all at once by cutting open her brain. There is no *all* before it comes into being—and when it does, often no one could have predicted its character.

What are we looking for when we demand that God be bigger than planet Earth, bigger than the entire evolutionary past and present of our species, and all its aspirations and accomplishments? That is vanity. It's like the joke about the man caught in a flood who climbs onto the roof of his house: A boat comes to rescue him, but he refuses, saying, "God will save me." Two more times rescuers arrive, but the man refuses them all, waiting for God to save him. Finally, as the water is going over his head, he cries out to God, "Why didn't you save me?" And God replies, "I sent three boats! What's your problem?"

Exactly. Why do we need the King of the Universe to get us off the roof?

God started small and simple, like everything in the universe and like the universe itself. Perhaps it happened when early humans began to share intentions and discovered they could cooperate to do something they could not do alone, something that they had nevertheless somehow imagined doing. Wondering what surrounded them, why they were here, and how they should live, our ancestors invented all kinds of means to share and express their answers, especially stories and symbols. From instant to instant, from then till now, the emerging God has been growing with the endless aspirations of the billions of us now around the planet. God doesn't exist outside the universe. It lives right here on Earth and connects all of us humans, not only to itself and to each other but to our ancestors. God is infinitely complex and ever expanding, but it has a direct relationship with every one of us.

The emerging God is radiating from every human on Earth, every book, every building and artifact, every plant grown by us, every shared endeavor, every mountaintop or galaxy that we have imbued with mythic significance. The kingdom of heaven is indeed spread upon the earth, but men do not see it because they're always looking up in the sky or at a sacred book. The emerging God is all around us and in us, and the more we learn, the more it feeds us. Some religions see God in the sky. Very old ones see gods in the earth out of which life arose. But God is in all the places that we humans have changed, improved, interpreted, and loved. And nowhere else.

When we look at the wars that have been fought over religion, it's clear that there is nothing we humans resist more passionately than changing our ideas of God. But for that very reason, there is nothing more liberating than the experience of actually doing so. The idea that God is universal is wrong on the science and destructive to society. If enough of us simply grasped that God cannot be literally universal, this alone would change the world.

The sacredness of God is not in its size but in its relationship to us.

We may not yet understand the mechanism by which God emerges, but the beauty of it is that this kind of question can be researched. Progress can be made. The emerging God can and should be a subject of scientific research—otherwise, how can anyone understand psychology, the social sciences, politics, history, or culture? God is a self-organizing phenomenon, and its organization is reflected in our cultures. The more we come to understand the connection between ourselves and God—that is, how an emergent phenomenon (God) continues to interact with its constituent sources (us)—the more we can *feel* that relationship and live on that exalted level.

The way God operates can't be guessed or intuited, because it must follow laws that emerge at a higher level of organization than we have mastered so far. As our understanding of emergence improves, we may be able to actually *discover* things about God, and any such discovery would be amazing. But we cannot ever come close to fully understanding God, because the more we try—the more we humans aspire to understand—the faster our aspirations expand God. God will always be light-years (and, with every instant that passes, more light-years) ahead of anything any one of us understands.

In *The God Delusion* the public atheist Richard Dawkins mocks theology as the only scholarly field without a subject. But there could be a theology that studies with scientific rigor how this unique phenomenon called God emerges from humanity collectively and what its ongoing influence is or can be on our behavior and our potential, both individually and worldwide, both at this moment and in the long run.

Here God is, hovering over the entire earth everywhere there are humans or human artifacts, touching each of our minds yet so beyond us in complexity and character that none of us has a prayer of ever fully understanding it. God contains tens of thousands of years of the planet's deepest thoughts—the truths of our ancestors' spoken and unspoken aspirations, integrated and raised to such a level of complexity that God emerged from them. God has grown with us and truly does shepherd us.

Or so we can see it, if we choose.

The biblical flat earth covered by a domed firmament is gone, and so is its God sitting on a mountaintop or cloud. The medieval earth at the center of the heavenly spheres is gone, and so is its God physically cradling the spheres. The Enlightenment picture of Earth as an average planet of an average star in the existential loneliness of infinite space is gone, and so is its God tucked away in a "spiritual realm" safe from Newton's laws. Those cosmologies are now history. We are building a new picture of our universe, of ourselves, and of our God. When we visualize our own highest aspirations as not only touching but being welcomed into God and instantly changing God's makeup, we can feel the electricity of this dynamic connection. A very real and Godlike emergent phenomenon burst from our distant ancestors, and its explosive power is available to us if we allow our minds to conceive of it.

God transcends us, but the universe transcends God. The moment we truly understand this and experience the reality of this relationship between, on the one hand, the planetary phenomenon of God and, on the other, the universe, everything becomes clear. God becomes intimately connected to every one of us yet is nevertheless awesome. The most important relationships in our lives are the close ones, not the distant ones. Why should it be different with God?

Knowing *what I am actually doing* when I connect to God is a large part of knowing *who I am*. And doing it stirs up excitement because I know I am truly connecting to something larger than myself or my imagination, larger than the entire human species back through prehistory, yet absolutely real.

Aspiring *is* connecting. It's so much easier than people think.

WHY DO WE NEED A NEW GOD?

Why should a new idea of God work better than just relying on science and leaving out the loaded word *God*? Why can't "phenomenon that emerged from collective human aspirations" be its own concept without being called God? It can. I'm not saying that using the name *God* is required, because it isn't. The question ultimately is not what we call it but whether we recognize the immense power that this emergent phenomenon has over us and all our ancestors and descendants. It needs a name. What name can best communicate its scale, meaning, and potential?

Right now every person on the face of this earth who is older than two or three has some concept of God. Since, as neuroscientists say, "neurons that fire together wire together," thought patterns repeated again and again, especially those that begin in early childhood, become hardwired into the brain. Consequently notions of God are not optional removable thoughts; rather, after tens of thousands of years of human cultural immersion, they're *physically embodied* in the cells of our brains. God is arguably the single most powerful concept in our minds. Everyone has some ideas about God, whether they see God as a comfort, a threat, a joy, a mystery, a symbol, an annoyance, or a delusion. But today this wide range of attitudes is, at least in Western religions, almost entirely focused on an impossible understanding of a being that intentionally created the universe and was whole and complete eons before any conscious or even living beings existed.

Seeing the power of God entirely through fictions divides our species at a time when cooperation is the only way we will be saved.

Meanwhile this other being has emerged from humanity itself and is absolutely real yet remains nameless and unrecognized. That nameless being is the one worthy of the name *God*. Perhaps there is some completely God-free big picture that could awaken a new sense of wholeness and participation and a new level of global cooperation, but I wouldn't bet on it. If we would just reexamine what we mean by God, we would not have to live bereft of its power.

Of course, you can't just choose a God for logic or convenience and actually believe in it—it has to work in your life before it will convince you. To be worthy of the name, the emerging God still has to do for us the essential things that the divine has always done. Give us hope and confidence and a big new perspective. Nurture our aspirations. Open our minds and hearts so we can feel our deep ties to each other, to other living creatures, to the planet we share and perhaps to some special place on it, and to the future. Inspire our personal quest for meaning and bravery in an often frightening world. Give us common ground. Less than that is not worthy of being called God. More than that is unnecessary.

Radical? Let's face reality. We in the modern world need a gigantic transformation of outlook to preserve our planet in a way that will preserve us. Science alone won't save the world. It can't even resist the backward-pulling religious dogmas, let alone inspire nonscientists. How does science help the great majority of us to *participate* in this universe? It doesn't. And if we don't *feel* we're participating, how can we understand the amazing ways that we are? How will we even know what we're missing? The mostly invisible double dark universe is so counterintuitive that we can't participate unless we understand what it means to do so. Understanding and participating are yin and yang, both equally necessary, but science gives us only yin. That's a lot. But it's not enough.

We humans are heading into troubled times, times of increasing conflict and chaos as the depleted resources of our planet get divided unfairly among a global population that is rapidly increasing—not only in numbers but in expectations per person. Meanwhile a destabilized climate has in many places already begun to randomly kill. We, the human species, are going to need every advantage we can muster to get through the transition to a sustainable civilization. It's no longer us against them, where "them" is other people: it's our species against the laws of nature, and nobody beats the laws of nature. The only winning strategy—the only true spiritual wisdom—is to figure out how to live in harmony with others on the planet that we share.

We all share the emerging God the same way we all share DNA. Contemplating a God that is *real in this universe* automatically awakens an awareness of the long term and the large scale. It nourishes the still-vital aspiration of our species to learn our true origin story—not as homework but because "from thence cometh my help." If enough people understood this, from thence could come an enormously heartening increase not only in our personal happiness and peace of mind but in the probability of our species' survival.

The great twentieth-century rabbi Abraham Joshua Heschel taught that God's role is not to be a comfort but a challenge. "Mankind will not perish for want of information," he wrote, "but only for want of appreciation. The beginning of our happiness lies in the understanding that life without wonder is not worth living." It's impossible to appreciate the wonder of this universe if we keep distorting its reality to allow it to have been designed by a fictional intelligence. It's also impossible to appreciate the miracle of our own existence if we keep denying or minimizing humanity's cosmic role in order to give all credit to that fiction. And it's impossible to appreciate the emerging planetary God unless we demand that our spiritual abilities and our scientific knowledge support each other. The divine challenge is to accept the evidence and become open to the possibility of a God that is real.

I have a mental image of our planetary God. Of course it's just an image, but it helps me feel it more closely. I visualize God as being like the oxygen in the atmosphere (a very ancient connection, actually, since one of the oldest names for God was the Hebrew *ruach*, or breath). Early Earth had almost no oxygen in the atmosphere. It was microbes that for billions of years exhaled as a waste product almost every molecule of oxygen in Earth's atmosphere. As the oxygen level of the atmosphere reached about 20 percent, it energized the evolution of all the higher creatures—possibilities that had never existed before. I see God as a cultural oxygen, endlessly emerging from us humans everywhere (yes, we're the microbes in this metaphor). God is our "meaningsphere," and no one who is conscious can fail to breathe it, any more than we can fail to breathe air.

Something real hovers among us. We can sense it with whatever tool we use to sense love or hope or when we catch our breath with wonder or possibility or gratitude at another human being's act, even one we're watching online. We draw from this meaningsphere all the time. Religion, mythology, and science are its collective creations.

God is an ever-growing being yet exists only because of us.

What a blessing to be free of the need to justify suffering as something God allows for His own reasons. Has something terrible ever happened to you or to someone you love? God had nothing to do with it. God doesn't control events. God influences how we see the events and interpret them. God doesn't control whether people get sick. God influences how our community understands illness and responds to it. God is a collective phenomenon—and yet it is also us. It's made of us. All our aspirations flow into it, without exception, and have been watering it since we lived in caves. God doesn't favor some people over others. God can no more discriminate among us than gravity can. God is in perpetual dialog with all of us.

It's a two-way street, like ants and their colony. Ants collectively build and run the colony, but the age and size of the colony affect what each individual ant experiences and therefore responds to.

It's not so different for us. We humans continually build God. But the aspirations of earlier humans created our world before we were born, so what the emerging God already is when we arrive affects what our generation experiences. One place we humans differ from the ants is in the limited lifetime of an ant colony. We intelligent beings could have another *billion* years on this planet, if we survive our reckless adolescence.

Once we know what God is, it's so much easier to perceive. It is truly awe inspiring—but it has emerged from a single species on a single planet of the billions of planets in our galaxy. Alien beings are often imagined as having fabulous technology or fabulously evil intentions, but who has ever imagined what their aspirations may be? What kind of god would the laws of physics, complexity, and evolution create in those beings, with their unknown (to us) aspirations? We may never be able to determine whether alien gods exist for aliens, but that is no excuse for not considering the possibility that they might—all over the universe. And somewhere in the very, very distant future, some new emergent phenomenon might even arise from all those gods interacting. If I take this possibility seriously, it eliminates any need for my God to be universal.

God arose from our distant ancestors like a flame bursting from dry wood that has reached the temperature of combustibility. Like fire—like all powers that humans exploit—the emerging God can be used harmfully or divinely. If we use it to save not just our individual selves but our children and grandchildren, our species, and our cosmic jewel of a planet, we shift the balance from harm toward divinity.

The moment we start thinking of God this way, a path appears out of the confusion of God images and their clash with the realities of science and the demands of modern life. There is a way both to peace of mind and inspiration. The implications are everywhere, and I pursue them in the chapters that follow.

PART II

CHAPTER 4

Is There a Spiritual World?

The word *spiritual* means many things to many people, so let me define it as simply as possible at the outset. *Spiritual*, as I use it, refers to *the experience of connecting to the larger reality we believe exists.* Spirituality is an experience, a sense of participating in something larger, but the experience is shaped by what a person believes that larger reality is, so spirituality will be different for different people.

And what is a spiritual world?

For some people the spiritual world is the location of their beloved dead, for others the place you finally get cosmic justice, for still others a land of mystical powers or beings. It may be separate from but equal to physical reality, it may be beyond the physical world—a special reality that transcends the physical universe. The very thought may be comforting, frightening, or ridiculous.

But no matter how people visualize the spiritual world or whether they believe that what they're visualizing actually exists, they make the same assumption: that *whatever* the spiritual world may be, it's not physical—that is, its events don't have to follow the laws of physics.

If we assume this, then the answer to the question of whether a spiritual world exists must be no: there could be no spiritual world except as an idea, and I could end the chapter here.

But what happens if we don't make that assumption? What if we accept that if the spiritual world is real, it must follow the laws of physics? We could ask: Is it possible that *in our universe* there is a spiritual world?

This time the answer can be yes—although the spiritual world may not be what you expect.

What is this statement based on? Scientific cosmology has zero to say about anything spiritual. The word doesn't even exist in the field. But scientific cosmology has blown open the meaning of *physical*, so that the concept of physical has a fascinating and unexpected relationship with the spiritual. The closest metaphor I can find to illustrate this relationship comes from the ancient world.

To the ancient Egyptians there was, as I discussed in chapter 1, no clear separation between the spiritual and the physical. The waters of the Nile flowed from the spiritual realm onto farms. People came from the spiritual realm and returned there after death. And as there was no clear line between the physical and the spiritual, there was no clear line between the *time* of the gods and the time of humans. The myths were literally about the doings of the gods at the beginning of time, but they were always symbolic of what was going on in the present. There was also no clear line between gods and humans. The pharaoh was not just a king. He was the god Horus. The Egyptians mentally lived in a world that was immersed in, and had been handed down to them from, the spiritual world, and their world *blended outward* into the spiritual world.

In medieval Christian Europe, there was a similar understanding that spiritual reality—heaven—engulfed the physical universe; it lay just outside the sphere of the stars. This view ended with Newton, because in the Newtonian picture (where Earth is not the stable center of the universe but a moving planet) the universe beyond the solar system was assumed to be physical reality governed by Newton's laws all the way out, perhaps to infinity.

Our modern picture of the double dark universe is closer to the ancient understanding than to the Newtonian. What we call physical today blends outward into the spiritual.

Perhaps the clearest way to understand the interplay between physical and spiritual that lets the spiritual world exist inside our universe is through an illustration. I want to make clear that once we accept the scientific premises that allow God to be real in this universe, the spiritual world can also be real—if we think about it in a coherent way.

The graphic below is based on the ancient symbol of a serpent swallowing its tail, called an *uroboros*, the Greek word for tail swallowing. For thousands of years cultures around the world have independently chosen the uroboros to represent some concept that was cosmic to them. From medieval Norse legends to the Huichol Indians of northern Mexico, the uroboros represented the horizon of the world, while to the Gnostics and others it represented the endlessness of time. The uroboros was first repurposed to symbolize the modern universe when the Nobel Prize–winning physicist Sheldon Glashow sketched it on a napkin in the early 1980s. Shortly thereafter my husband and I began using the image to teach college students, and then we developed it to communicate more and more of what we know about the new picture of the universe. We call our version the Cosmic Uroboros. It represents the modern scientific universe as *the range of all possible sizes*.

The head of the serpent represents the largest size science can know anything about—the size of our visible universe, about 10^{29} centimeters in radius (a centimeter is about two-fifths of an inch). The visible universe is a finite size because it began a certain length of time ago and has been expanding ever since, so the size it's grown to in that time is the largest size we can say anything meaningful about: approximately 46 billion light-years in radius. That's how far the material that emitted the heat radiation of the Big Bang is from us now. That's the largest size. (The universe is only 13.8 billion years old, but remember that it has been expanding ever since, and for the past five billion years it has been expanding at an accelerating rate—that's why its radius is so much bigger than 13.8 billion light-years.)

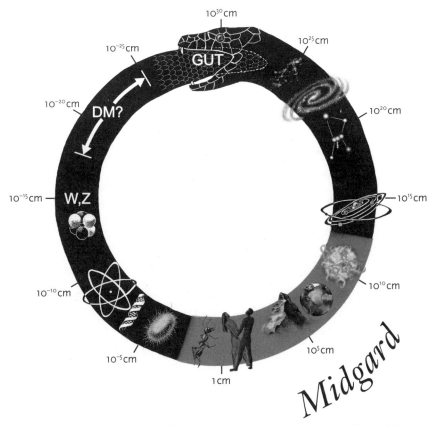

Figure 4. The Cosmic Uroboros: the modern universe as the range of all possible sizes.

At the opposite extreme the tip of the serpent's tail represents the smallest size permitted by the known laws of physics. There's a smallest size because, according to general relativity, there can't be more than a certain amount of mass squeezed into a defined region. If more mass is packed in than the region can hold, gravity there becomes so intense that the region itself—the space—collapses to no size at all. This is a black hole. Nothing can escape from inside a black hole, not even light, hence the term. Any object compressed enough will hit this limit and suddenly become a black hole.

Meanwhile quantum mechanics sets the minimum size limit in a different way. Electrons, protons, and other particles have extremely small masses and are always whizzing about. They are hard to pinpoint. The size of a particle is actually the size of the region in which you can confidently locate it. The smaller the region in which the particle is confined, the more energy it takes to find it, and more energy is equivalent to larger mass. There turns out to be a special small size where the *maximum* mass that relativity allows to be crammed in without the region's collapsing into a black hole is also the *minimum* mass that quantum mechanics allows to be confined in so tiny a region. That size, about 10^{-33} centimeters, is called the Planck length. We have no way to talk, or even think, about anything smaller in our current understanding of physics, so that's the smallest size.

All the sizes in between are arrayed along the serpent's body. At each tick mark we're looking at a size 100,000 times larger than the previous tick mark.

The head is more than 10^{60} times bigger than the tail. That's a one with sixty zeroes. For most of human history this astonishingly wide range of potential sizes was not only unknown but unimaginable and inexpressible. Even when people thought of the universe as infinite, all they really meant was "like what we know, extending forever"—an unimaginative concept compared to 10^{60}.

But the truly amazing thing is that all the universe's exotically large and small size scales have now been discovered. In pure mathematics the powers of ten go on infinitely but not in the physical world. The Cosmic Uroboros is *complete*. We have a picture of the universe as a whole.

This may sound counterintuitive, but in different locations along the Cosmic Uroboros—that is, on different size scales—*different laws of physics* control events. The laws of physics are all always true, but they don't always matter. For example, electromagnetic forces (the basis of chemistry) hold matter together from atoms up to mountains, even though gravity also plays a role. But around the size scale of mountains, gravity starts to gain the upper hand over electromagnetism. A competition between electromagnetism and gravity determines the maximum height of mountains. When the mountain becomes big enough, its gravity overcomes the electromagnetic forces that hold the material of the mountain together, and the roots of the mountain flow or break, causing earthquakes. The smaller the mass of a planet, the weaker the force of gravity pulling the mountain down. So mountains can be much higher on smaller planets like Mars than they can be on Earth.

When we delve into sizes smaller than an atom, like the size scale of the nucleus of the atom, electromagnetism again finds major competition, but it's not from gravity this time. Gravity is of no importance at all on these scales. You can ignore it. In fact, gravity's power fades out much earlier. You can drop a mouse down a thousand-yard mine shaft and at the bottom, so long as the ground is soft, it will walk away. Gravity plays no role in the life of bacteria or anything smaller. At subatomic scales electromagnetism loses its power to what are called the strong and weak interactions. An atomic nucleus is made of positively charged protons (plus neutral neutrons) bunched together. Positive charges should repel each other, but their mutual (electromagnetic) repulsion is overcome by the strong force, which holds the nucleus together. But the range of the strong force is too short to have any effect beyond the atom.

What happens when we go clockwise along the Cosmic Uroboros to much, much smaller sizes, to the very tip of the tail? Gravity suddenly becomes extremely powerful again, because its strength increases as objects get closer to each other, and at the tip of the tail distances between particles are almost unimaginably small. The Cosmic Uroboros swallows its tail because tail swallowing represents the idea that gravity may be the link between largest and smallest and the force that unifies the universe.

Where do we humans fit into this grand scheme of things? We are almost exactly at the center. On the Cosmic Uroboros each of us is midway between the size of a living cell and the size of Earth. We are midway between an atom and a star and midway between the largest and the smallest sizes. If you ever hear anyone say that looking up at a starry sky makes them feel small or insignificant, gently remind them that we're not small at all: we are at the center of all possible sizes.

There is just as much universe within us as there is without.

Our central location on the Cosmic Uroboros is the sweet spot for complex intelligence—it's the size that's big enough to be made of a huge number and variety of atoms but small enough so that the cosmic speed limit (the speed of light) doesn't interfere in the slightest with our internal communications, like thinking. Since nothing can travel faster than the speed of light, a creature that was much larger than we are would, even if it thought at maximal speed, think more slowly the larger it was. (Our actual speed of thought is quite a bit slower than the speed of light, since it depends not only on electrical impulses but also on chemicals called neurotransmitters that actually move between neurons.)

If the reasons that we humans are central were based in biology, those reasons might be limited to us here on Earth. But the reasons are based in physics, which is the same everywhere in the universe, so they apply equally to intelligent life on any world. Intelligent aliens, if they exist, must be close to our central size—that is, somewhere between a redwood tree and a puppy. Which is actually a narrow range, given the possibilities of this universe.

Every phenomenon or creature has its place in the range of sizes on the Cosmic Uroboros and could not exist much larger or much smaller. An ancient Chinese conundrum says, "Last night I dreamed I was a butterfly. Or am I a butterfly today dreaming that I am a man?" Now we know the answer. A butterfly can't dream it's a man unless it's mentally complex enough to understand what it is to be a man, and this means the dreamer is a human. Science fiction notwithstanding, there can't be giant insects the size of a truck, and you can't shrink the kids. Size is destiny.

OUR PLACE IN THE UNIVERSE

Of all the sizes possible in the cosmos, there is one size range that is special for beings like us. It's the light section of the serpent's body in figure 4. This is the range of sizes—from the tiniest creature visible to the naked eye up to maybe the sun—that contains everything humans have always been able to see. In this range of sizes our good old Earth-based intuition can be reliable. We can name that special range of sizes Midgard. Midgard is not a place; it's a setting of our mental zoom lens.

In the Old Norse mythology Midgard represented the human world of civilized society. Midgard was visualized as an island in the middle of the "world-sea," which represented the Norse universe. Far across the world-sea from Midgard in one direction lay the land of the giants and in the opposite direction lay the land of the gods.

Our special size range on the Cosmic Uroboros is, like Midgard, an island in the middle of the size scales of the universe; it's the narrow range of sizes that are familiar to us and that have shaped human consciousness and intuition throughout our evolution. But with the benefit of science we now know that on the Cosmic Uroboros beyond the shores of Midgard in one direction—outward, counterclockwise, into the expanding universe—lies the land of incomprehensibly giant beings, like black holes a billion times the mass of the sun and galaxies made of hundreds of billions of stars. In the opposite direction from Midgard—inward, toward the small—lies a living cellular world and, within that, the quantum world. These microlands may not be gods, but they're the evolutionary and physical sources of everything we are.

Every size scale holds a different world. Every world, when you focus on it, appears to be not a size scale but reality itself.

A thought experiment can help to break out of our limited Earth-based intuition, so here's one to help explore our connection to the size scales of the universe beyond Midgard.

> In your imagination, curl yourself up into a ball and become an atom in your body. Your electron cloud touches the electron clouds of the atoms all around you. The world of atoms is a cozy world.
>
> But now imagine that you, much more tightly curled up, are the nucleus of that atom. You look outward, but it is six miles to the next nucleus of your kind, and there is little comfort in knowing that three miles away its electron cloud is touching yours.
>
> Imagine now that you are a star. It is an even lonelier world. If you are standing on a mountaintop in California, your closest neighbor is in Australia. You are the only two people on Earth. Even if you are a star in a dense globular star cluster, your closest neighbor is a thousand miles away.
>
> Imagine now that you are a galaxy. Things become almost cozy again. Other galaxies are not far away. Your nearest neighboring galaxy is sitting only twenty feet away. If you are in a rich cluster of galaxies, your nearest neighbor is only a few feet away, and you feel like a person at a cocktail party. But conversation is virtually impossible. It takes 100,000 years for one thought to cross your galactic mind, and many times that to formulate an idea, because you are 100,000 light-years across and you can't think faster than the speed of light. You have barely had time for a few thoughts in the ten billion years that you have existed.

Thinking is the privilege of creatures like us, who live in Midgard. We are the Goldilocks size, small enough not to be bothered by the speed of light but big enough to be enormously complex—complex enough that we can perform thought experiments.

Using our Midgard intuition, we all have a good sense of what a physical object is: it's solid and measurable. Everyone agrees it's here. But as our minds move outside Midgard to explore other size scales using science, the concept of "physical" becomes progressively more metaphorical until at very large and very small scales it loses its meaning. For example, everyone who switches on a light knows electrons are real or there wouldn't be electricity. But is an individual electron a physical object? It's not literally a particle like a tiny marble; it's a probability that something is happening. The probability is what's confirmed experimentally and thus is real. Is a probability a physical object?

On the large scale is a supercluster of galaxies a physical object? A supercluster can be a sheet of maybe ten thousand large galaxies and many smaller ones, but the sheet is being torn apart by the wildly expanding space inside it. We can't see this happening, though, because a supercluster is so huge (10^{25} centimeters on the Cosmic Uroboros) that the tearing apart will take billions of years.

Imagine that you are a supercluster of galaxies. You are touching the next supercluster, and it touches the next, like people holding hands and encircling large voids. But your consciousness is barely flickering, because unlike a galaxy you are not bound together by gravity. Your parts are expanding away from each other. In time you will drift apart like clouds in a blue sky. You're not really "something" except in human beings' dot-connecting minds—yet what you are may last far longer than planet Earth.

Is a supercluster a physical object?

What we mean in ordinary discourse by the word *physical* turns out to be utterly irrelevant to most of the universe. In fact, the phrase "physical universe" is an oxymoron, since so much of the universe is not what we normally mean by physical, even though it's governed by laws of physics. "Physical" is a clear and meaningful characteristic only of things in the size range of Midgard. It may be the defining characteristic of Midgard.

What is the rest of the universe if it's not physical?

The rest of the Cosmic Uroboros is the spiritual realm to us. We can have no direct sensory contact with electrons or superclusters—our sensory awareness works only in Midgard. Outside Midgard lie exotic size scales that are mentally accessible through science but whose events are not physical in the Earth-intuitive sense. *Midgard is surrounded by the spiritual world.*

Where is God on the Cosmic Uroboros?

God is not the objects along the serpent, not the atoms, humans, stars, or galaxies; it's the conceptual framework that holds them together and gives meaning to our universe.

WHY DOES THIS MATTER?

The spiritual world for scientifically literate people does not have to be some nether realm or escape fantasy. As we let our consciousness spread outward from Midgard along the Cosmic Uroboros into the larger and smaller scales of reality, we revitalize in a modern way the ancient experience of being surrounded by the spiritual world with no clear dividing line between it and the physical reality of Earth. We can use the metaphor of the serpent to send our consciousness far beyond all earlier cultures' spiritual horizons to see, in the mind's eye, the entire Cosmic Uroboros. The new understanding of our cosmic place at the center of all possible sizes is grounded in scientific knowledge, but our experience, our sense that we are present and part of this universe, can only be called spiritual.

This matters because we don't fully understand how we fit into the universe if we don't *feel* that we are part of it. Feelings don't tell us what's true, but they do tell us what we believe. If we don't believe that we're part of this universe, then we have missed the point—that this universe is real.

Most of the universe is spiritual but only if we remember what those words mean. If people ever slip back into prescientific fantasy and shadows and forget this new cosmology, the spiritual world will disappear like a lost Eden.

Most of the scientific universe is spiritual! We should be shouting this from the rooftops. We have the choice today to see reality as it truly is, to the best of our collective ability. If we draw creatively from the ocean of metaphors in our minds to connect our feelings more intimately with what we now understand; if we share the knowledge and wisdom we have been bequeathed by brave and brilliant explorers who have gone before us and are even now serving us; if we open our minds willingly and exuberantly to a real God in the real universe, we will find that there is indeed a spiritual world. We live in its physical core, but the emerging God has made it possible to see the whole.

CHAPTER 5

Does God Answer Prayers?

This is a question *about* God. Talking about God and talking to God differ by only a preposition, but they are completely different activities. They're even done on opposite sides of the brain. There's no need to know much about God or to be able to describe God in words in order to pray and find comfort in doing so. But the kind of comfort you can find that way has to be compartmentalized from much of the rest of modern life. The problem is, protecting God in a compartment separate from most of daily life pushes *away* from the possibility of sacredness most of what we spend our days doing. That feels bad much of the time and leads to incoherence. But our minds don't have to be split that way anymore.

For years I talked to God, even though I had no idea what I was talking to, if anything. Talking to God doesn't mean I think it's a person. Talking is how I establish my own feelings of connection. People talk to their cats and their plants but don't necessarily think the cats or plants understand. I even spoke to a budgie and a goldfish when I had them. Neither understood me, and I didn't expect them to pipe up. That wasn't the point. I was enjoying my own feelings toward them. Talking helps us humans *experience* our connections to each other, and evolutionarily language has been fantastically effective at nurturing relationships. According to the anthropologist Robin Dunbar in his wonderful book *Gossip, Grooming, and the*

Evolution of Language, nonhuman primates establish closeness by grooming each other, carefully combing through and picking nits and burrs out of each other's fur. But this is time consuming; each individual can groom only a few others. Early humans learned to establish closeness by talking as well. We can talk to several people at a time. Talking continually enlarges the circle of bonding. If I want to feel and cultivate my connection to God or the universe, I want to use the most highly evolved ability I have for connecting—language.

But why should I want to connect this way to God? Because one day I was at an event with a beautiful buffet. It was about three o'clock on a Sunday afternoon, not mealtime for me, but everything looked delicious and everyone else was digging in lustily. I could feel myself starting to tear apart inside: part of me wanted to taste everything, and part of me lived in fear that I would. The tension was starting to distract me from the people I had come to be with. Then out of the blue it occurred to me to ask for help. Now, at that period I was asking for help almost every day, largely to no avail. I thought praying was something you did in the morning, like showering. I had not really done it seriously once temptation was already hovering, because the pull of temptation was always more attractive. But this time I did. I asked at the very turning point when the food was calling its loudest and I was within inches of reaching for it. I stopped and took a moment to pray for help. I gave peace of mind a chance. And suddenly I felt a kind of soft pleasure and cleanliness. The struggle disappeared. Without the slightest feeling of temptation and without having to talk myself out of it, I simply walked away from the laden table like a boat gliding through calm water. I had never experienced that before. This was the feeling that kept me coming back—this extraordinary pleasure in taking care of myself without doubt, struggle, or excuses. Where did it come from? How could praying to something I didn't actually believe existed do this? I drew a blank.

When I don't pray, I tend to stay at a default level or even sink into my own worst habits. No aspirations there. Aspirations need to be cultivated, nurtured, buoyed, reinforced. They are not automatic. When I pray, I'm consciously placing myself in the upward flow of the best of humanity. In the end I not only improve my own behavior in a way guided by that prayer but—because I am a tributary, however tiny, to the general level of human aspirations—I also automatically uplift our whole species. And this uplifts God.

But prayers that uplift can't depend on ruled-out beliefs. If, for example, I prayed for a violation of the laws of nature (God, make the hurricane turn away!) even for the most selfless reason, that would not uplift our species but drag it down into ignorance. Those who assume prayer can't work are often equating prayer with requests like this for magical intercession in the world. This kind of prayer, they are right, will not be answered—not because it's a prayer but because it's based on rejecting reality. If it seems to be answered—if the hurricane changes course or a parking place suddenly appears— it's a coincidence. But a prayer that helps us accept and navigate reality and our deepest needs can be a tool for self-empowerment, just as rational thinking is a tool for self-empowerment.

It has taken me much longer to be able to talk *about* God than to talk *to* God, but in this chapter I want to explore how they fit together. How can we come to feel that praying is not just talking to ourselves, that there is one reality, the emerging God is part of it, and so are we? I don't want to be compartmentalized. I don't want one side of my brain not to know what the other is doing. I don't want that constant low-level tension of addiction that is repeatedly seducing me toward what I don't want, like an abused woman returning to her abuser.

Participating in this universe can feel either like fulfillment or boredom, pleasure or numbness, depending on how we *think* about it. This is why it matters so much to have a coherent way to think about God. We live out our participation, but we live *in* it more deeply by praying. How well we succeed in finding the fulfillment and pleasure in this cosmos, rather than boredom and numbness, depends on whether we have metaphors that help us.

The emerging God is not a supernatural being who listens or possesses a will, desires, or decision-making ability. So how can such a God help us?

Can it love us?

Can we love it?

Can it respond?

Can it answer our prayers?

The answers to the last four questions are yes, yes, yes, and yes. The answer to the first is that the answers to the last four are yes, yes, yes, and yes.

But words must be interpreted. We have to keep reorienting ourselves in the new universe, never assuming that we know what baggage-burdened words may mean in this new context.

WHO IS LISTENING?

If no all-powerful God is out there listening to prayers and weighing whom to help and whom to ignore, it's nevertheless the case that no one prays alone. Something is listening. That may sound paradoxical but only within the commonsense world.

Praying has always been a way of establishing a relationship and strengthening and finding comfort in it. A relationship between what and what? On one side it's you or me who is praying.

But on the other side . . . what?

On the other side there is a *larger consciousness than what we think of as our own*. Millions of people intuit this but then assume that the larger consciousness belongs to a separate God. Or they think of it *as* God. But projecting it completely outside ourselves causes confusion and incoherence, because no larger consciousness could be floating in space *independent* of intelligent beings.

Then where could this larger consciousness be? Let's look at the actual possibilities. What's out there? In a universe filled with dark matter and dark energy, traces of stardust exist, rare as gold in a mountain. Consciousness, large or small, can be generated only by *something made of stardust*, because stardust is the only ingredient in this universe that can engage in chemical interactions so intricate that consciousness can emerge from them.

Stardust, remember, means the hundred or so kinds of atoms that get blown out of stars when the stars explode or die some other violent death. The stars themselves are mainly made of hydrogen and helium, the two primeval atoms that came straight out of the Big Bang. Condensing into stars, hydrogen and helium start fusing together into heavier atoms and are thus the parents of oxygen, carbon, silicon, iron, nitrogen, and all other stardust atoms.

During its entire lifetime a star converts only the tiniest bit of its mass into stardust. Stardust is only *one-hundredth of one percent* of the density of the universe. It's by far the rarest of all the cosmic ingredients. Yet our bodies are 90 percent stardust by weight (the rest is hydrogen, mostly in our H_2O). The emergence of our kind of consciousness could happen only in a Fort Knox of stardust, like Earth.

Astronomers are notoriously conservative and still refer to stardust as ordinary matter (as opposed to dark matter). But from a cosmic perspective what's ordinary is dark matter, which is 27 percent of the density of the universe. Stardust, at 0.01 percent, is extraordinary matter.

But matter itself is the little guy in the universe. It's dwarfed by the dark energy, the energy causing the expansion of the universe to keep accelerating. Dark energy is 69 percent of the density of the universe, and that percentage will keep growing, perhaps forever. (Energy has density because it can be expressed as mass, which is the meaning of $E = mc^2$.) But although dark matter and dark energy together utterly dominate the universe in size, power, and longevity, they can never achieve consciousness because they can never become complex enough. Earth is a flourishing oasis of consciousness in the mindless desert of space, and no one knows how far it is to the next oasis.

Among the conscious critters on Earth, which may include all of them, self-consciousness is exceedingly rare. It took the universe almost fourteen billion years to make the first little bit of it here. We self-conscious Earthlings are like diamonds inside Tiffany's—we look around and assume diamonds are common. There are whole drawers and display cases filled with us. But if we open our awareness to the world outside the store, we are struck by how rare and precious diamonds are in the larger context. Self-consciousness is like that: it's the diamond of the universe.

The "larger consciousness" to which we pray must be even more extraordinary than self-consciousness—but it can't be floating in the universe as a separate God.

It also can't be entirely inside any of us or it would simply be our own self-consciousness. As I described in the introduction, I arrived at this conclusion experimentally. There was a time in my recovery when I had actually made progress that was at least in part the result of my new practice of praying to a God whose existence I was acting as if I acknowledged. After what seemed at the time like a reasonable amount of thought, I decided intellectually that praying was a clever psychological strategy, addressed to myself. But as soon as I decided that, I began to lose my ability to pray. I became isolated spiritually. Food started calling out again, and I found myself thinking, "Why not? I don't care!" Then my powerlessness over food came back with a vengeance. Talking to God is not a theoretical exercise for people like me; it can have serious real-world consequences.

This scary experiment convinced me that a useful God can't be simply a thought in my mind. However, the external floating version of God also doesn't work. Nor can the larger consciousness be somewhere outside the universe, since if there even is such a place, nothing there could ever contact us, and we could never contact it. What does that leave?

Where is the larger consciousness?

LOCATING THE LARGER CONSCIOUSNESS

In chapter 4, I used the Cosmic Uroboros to represent all the sizes that things in the visible universe can physically be. I'm going to locate the larger consciousness with a metaphor based on that metaphor.

The Uroboros of Human Identity is a symbol that represents all the sizes of identity we humans possess, if only we would look. Each of us is an entire uroboros of roles we play on multiple size scales. The way our roles interact helps shape God. The serpent swallows its tail because each of us is a coherent self. Or we can be.

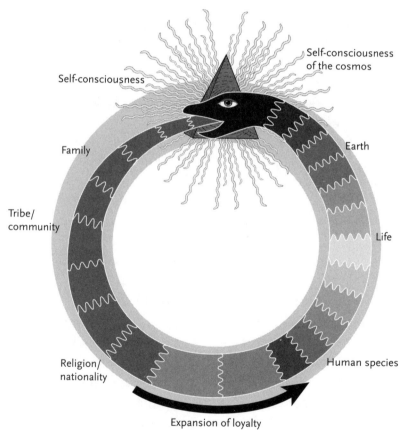

Figure 5. The Uroboros of Human Identity.

Each of us has an individual self-consciousness, represented by the tip of the tail. On increasingly larger size scales, we identify ourselves as part of a family, then of a tribe and/or community (or communities), and then of a religion or ethnicity and/or nation. But our deepest identities are far larger and much older than any culturally invented religion, ethnicity, or nation: we are human beings, we are life, we are Earth, and we are at least part of the self-consciousness of the universe.

Now we can identify the larger consciousness—because we can point to where it is: it's *spread along* the increasing size scales of the Uroboros of Human Identity.

The power of praying comes from daring to enter that mysterious place between the emerging God and us. But it's not an empty space—it's our own selves on progressively larger size scales, where we are participating in multiple emerging phenomena and creating emergent identities. As the ancient Egyptian world blended outward into the spiritual world, so does ours. And the higher our consciousness goes along the Uroboros of Human Identity, the more it blends into the emerging phenomenon of God. In tuning our ordinary consciousness in to those higher levels that we may have scarcely ever visited before, we approach God.

This may seem bizarre. How can size scales alone control such great mysteries? How can what's essentially a number have the most profound of spiritual impacts? Well, size is not just a number—size determines cosmic identity. The number that describes a size is not in itself important but is a powerful symbol of the complexity possible on that size scale. Size is a key to the universe. On the Cosmic Uroboros size distinguishes the physical from the spiritual. In fact, in this universe the size or complexity level of a thing or event determines not only its nature but which world it's operating in and which physical laws control that world.

But all these worlds exist all the time. And our minds now know it. We can't simply ignore this when we think about God. God fits into this very pattern by emerging.

Prayer is a conversation among different faces of ourselves as we exist on different size scales. We send our ordinary consciousness out to connect to our roles on emergent size scales. Those roles speak back to us if we're open to their existence. After all, that's us in there playing them. They expand our sense of self. Their messages sound like thoughts, but in some deep sense they actually are messages, because they come from outside our normal culture-stunted state of mind.

OUR GOD-CAPACITY

It's time to crack open the whole idea of talking to God. If we are in a universe now known to span more than sixty orders of magnitude, and God is emerging from the infinite interactions of human aspirations, we have to look at everything anew. We've already begun to do this intellectually, but can we do it emotionally? How can we step outside images of God that are many centuries deep and realize that those are only images and not reality?

It turns out all humans have a tool that will let us do this. The perfect name for it was suggested by the psychoanalyst Carl Jung. In an interview filmed in the early 1950s Jung was asked bluntly, "Do you believe God exists?" Earlier Jung had written that all people need ideas and convictions that can give meaning to their lives and help them find their "place in the universe" (his phrase). He had written that we have the *capacity* to satisfy this need symbolically with a god image. He answered the interviewer by saying, "What I know is that all humans have a 'god-capacity.'"

That's the tool. Our god-capacity.

Religions offer up symbols and images bounteously, but a capacity is something that belongs to us *as humans*, not as members of any religion. Our god-capacity is not tied to any specific tradition or symbol. It doesn't require any particular view of God. It's the ability to scratch the meaning-itch with a symbol.

Shouldn't we want that symbol to represent the highest truth we know?

Public atheists like Richard Dawkins and others assume that unless a supernatural God is out there, ready and willing to answer prayers, there is no point in praying, and since such a God does not exist, praying is self-delusion. To them our god-capacity is not an ability but a *liability*, because it leads people to believe in the objective reality of their fantasies.

Many people do indeed believe in the objective reality of their fantasies, and doing so can be wildly dangerous in this world, but trashing our god-capacity because some people do this is like trashing love because sometimes it goes wrong.

At this moment in history, what is the highest and best use of our god-capacity? That is, what is best both for ourselves as vulnerable human beings and for the planet upon which all our lives and all our purposes depend? Like any capacity, the god-capacity needs to be exercised or lost—and is crying out to be exercised as new knowledge comes in and new generations face a changing world. The god-capacity has been used historically for great good and great ill, and it's still capable of both. Only when we recognize that it belongs to us, not to any religion, will we realize that we could put it to much better use.

We have the power to change our images of God without losing God. This is what we need to do, given the knowledge now available, the needs we have, and the state of our world.

MORE THAN KNOWING: PARTICIPATING IN THE UNIVERSE

What almost everyone wants is to *participate fully* in a meaningful universe. People who have experienced a spiritual connection, or who have seen enough examples around them to know that it *can* be experienced, are sometimes willing to pay a heavy price to get it. Anyone who has ever written or avidly read fiction knows this. A character is attractive when she desperately wants something and commits herself to getting it. We want to see her milk life for all it's worth. We want to see other people's aspirations. That's what makes them matter. That's why we like strong bad characters better than weak good ones. What matters is to be *alive*. Not to live by half-measures.

In her intriguing book *When God Talks Back*, the Stanford anthropologist T. M. Luhrmann reports on her study of a group of evangelical Christians. She wanted to understand how sensible people can believe in an invisible, imperceptible being who, as she puts it, "gives none of the ordinary signs of existence." How can they actually hear their God speaking to them like a person standing next to them, comforting them or giving them warnings or suggestions? What Luhrmann argues is that hearing God talk this way is not, contrary to many outsiders' assumptions, a crazy belief; it's a *skill* that the evangelicals work hard to master. They train their minds to interpret signs and feelings as communications from God and to think of God as a person who loves and speaks to them. They reinforce this picture of reality with the kind of language they use every time they talk to each other.

These are modern people with doubts like anyone else about whether God could actually be standing next to them, but their overwhelming desire to feel a spiritual connection sidelines these doubts. The evangelicals who train their minds in this way have committed themselves to feeling like true participants in the larger reality they believe exists, no matter how hard it may be—but the reason it's so hard is that their metaphor communicates the wrong "reality."

"They learn to reinterpret the familiar experiences of their own minds and bodies as not being their own at all—but God's," Luhrmann writes.

They learn to identify some thoughts as God's voice, some images as God's suggestions, some sensations as God's touch or the response to his nearness. . . . They [map] the abstract concept "God" out of their mental awareness into a being they imagine and reimagine *in ways shaped by the Bible and encouraged by their church community*. (Emphasis is mine.)

And there lies the problem: it's not that they hear God speak but that they work so hard to hear only from a biblical God. They're putting all this heartfelt energy and dedication and love into experiencing a prescientific metaphor instead of the reality they're actually living in.

But the mind training they do could be tremendously valuable and admirable if it were aimed at a different metaphor. Evangelicals have something incredibly important to teach the rest of us, because if it's possible to train the mind to experience what is not there, then surely it is possible to train the mind to experience what *is* there. It's probably easier, because there's no need to struggle against the evidence.

Just believe the evidence.

As humans on planet Earth we don't get to choose what reality is, but we get to discover it and, if we're very lucky, participate fully in it. It is what it is. The question for us is whether we recognize it and come to love it and the way that taking our place in it makes us feel—or whether we instead curl up inside the comfort of old stories and shut out the universe and much of the modern scientific world. There's nothing like the feeling of fitting smoothly into reality to soothe the torn parts and create peace of mind.

So far hardly anybody has accurate concepts for grasping the spiritual meaning of what lies beyond Midgard. We've inherited our notions of the universe from people whose idea of beyond started just a few miles from home and whose God was a lord or king or father. Basically, a man. Science is providing new metaphors that make it possible to use our god-capacity in a new way: to participate in the real universe. Not just to know our place in the universe but to *fill it*. To be it.

There is a God that's closer to every one of us than the air we breathe and more powerful than the zeitgeist in which our lives are planted. If we could learn from the evangelicals how to feel as though we're really in touch with the emerging God in the ways we actually are, we could experience the joy and awe of participation in the universe and see the possibility of prayer as a cosmic blessing.

We have learned from the evangelicals in Luhrmann's study that if we are motivated enough, it's possible to train our minds to experience *whatever we believe* is real. What if we directed toward the real universe and the emerging God even a fraction of the effort that millions of religious people make every day to experience the presence of their image of God?

The techniques that religious people have developed are free for adaptation and redirection. We too can seek to participate in the real universe and try to imagine in our own expanding consciousness what the emerging God might say, if it could speak. This kind of training could be a great leap not just for consciousness but also for conscience, because the God emerging from humanity speaks for humanity, not for my political party or your country. When we start to think from humanity's point of view, we can't put our private interests first. We see the big picture and we see from it. The God that's truly present is not a person, so we won't be hearing it speak to us like a person, but we can feel its presence as it embraces us deep in our brains and emotions and unveils its perspective.

We can *count* on a God that is real.

We can use our god-capacity to experience the miracle of our own universe up close and to hear it speak to us through the God that is emerging from the collective. If we draw on our god-capacity to absorb and resonate with this idea of an emerging God, we'll discover that praying can be powerful. When we pray as a way of unearthing or strengthening our own aspirations, we're participating in one of the most creative acts a person can do: conjuring up the best in ourselves, sometimes better bests than we ever consciously thought possible.

When we listen for the perspective of the emerging God, we're putting ourselves in that great river of power that animates the human race and thus ourselves. It's like a stethoscope: there's no magic in it—it focuses us and frees our consciousness of distractions.

Prayer can be something creative and wonderful. It's always been a reaching-out to whatever larger reality people believed or hoped existed. We can reach a lot further now. In fact, one of the greatest experiences of life is to flow in both directions along the uroboros as far as possible but to love our special nook in the expanding universe.

CONTEMPLATING THE UNIVERSE CAN BE PRAYING

It's often said that prayer is talking to God and meditation is listening for the answer. That can be true, of course, but it's not the only way. If we meditate on how the universe works *as if we actually believed it*, that would be a prayer to reality, and reality is the parent of God and everything else. This kind of prayer is a way of harmonizing oneself with the reality that can host an emerging God. We no longer live in an intuitive universe, but most of our words still refer to earthly experiences and, unless we unchain them as metaphors, these metaphors mislead us to think that they accurately reflect reality. If we want to know how to talk to God, or how God might talk to us, we need to train our minds to live in the same universe as God. Doing so can be prayer.

For example, all educated people today believe, correctly, that the sun doesn't actually set; it's Earth that's turning. Yet hardly anyone *experiences* being on a rotating planet. It's as if they know it but can't believe it. But with a little imagination, it's easy. Read the following paragraph as slowly as you can.

Imagine you are lying on your back in the soft grass late on a warm spring afternoon, your feet toward the south, looking up at the sky.

Spread out your arms and legs and feel the earth below you. You have nowhere to go. You are just a part of the earth. As the day is ending, slowly turn your head to the right and look west toward the reddening sun. Feel your patch of Earth turning away from the sun, heading into night. Just as the horizon on your right rises to meet the sun, turn your head all the way left. There you see on the eastern horizon the moon, huge and orange, appearing at precisely the moment of sunset. Tonight is the night of the full moon, when sun and moon are in perfect balance. It was in many cultures a night of power. Feel your patch of ground moving slowly toward the moon. The haze of atmosphere through which you saw the moon as you looked across the surface of the planet is moving out of the line of sight. The moon appears to rise and become whiter because you're seeing it through less and less atmosphere. It seems smaller but only because it is no longer near the horizon and your mind no longer compares it with familiar objects in the earthly landscape. Let time pass. Let Earth carry you around until the last glow of sunlight disappears and stops masking the stars. You have traveled into night with your planet. You *are* the side of the planet traveling into night.

If you read that slowly enough to feel you were there, then you just prayed, because you brought your consciousness into alignment with the reality where God can be found. We're often taught that imagination is the opposite of reality, but it's not that simple. It takes a lot of imagination to see cosmic reality. But not any old kind of imagination: imagining needs to be *disciplined* by knowledge of what's not possible and catalyzed by new concepts that suggest what might be. We've all said at one time or another, "Anything is possible!" but people who truly believe it are most likely to imagine fantasies and miss most of reality.

We're truly participating in our universe when we come to feel in our bones that we are part of the story, thoroughly integrated into the big picture. God is emerging from us and bound into us, we know where we stand in the cosmos, and we know what we are.

This feeling has to be constantly reinforced and strengthened. One attempt at this kind of prayer won't change you but practicing will. Are you watching a gorgeous sunset? You could just enjoy the pretty scene, or you could use its dynamic beauty as a visceral reminder of where we are: we're immersed in Earth's transparent atmosphere, which is as thin as the skin on an apple, yet it's thick enough as we look sideways through it to redden the light of the sun.

It takes a little extra effort to visualize, true, but it's like the effort we all expended learning to read. Hasn't that paid off? Far from stripping the world of beauty, hasn't reading opened to all of us the many beauties and ideas that language can evoke? Can you imagine how much smaller and more fearful your existence would be if you could not read? It's the same with participating in our universe: we're smaller and more fearful if we don't know where we are and can't feel that we fit in.

Let's try a different experiment. Once again, read this as slowly as you can.

Imagine you have lost your memory. You stare at yourself in a mirror, but there is only this moment. You are unaware of any past. You see your reflection, you're solid, you're well dressed, your heart is pumping, but how you got to the spot on which you stand, you have no idea.

Who are you?

You're not your family background, your personal history, the work you've done, your hopes for the future. These don't exist. With no time dimension you're like a computer with hormones. You're listening to the latest music, wanting the coolest products, and taking as reality the latest media reports of the world outside your room. This is all you know.

Now imagine that you look into the mirror again, but instantly you see through the momentary you of today back to the you of years ago, to the child you once were, then the toddler. Let your consciousness fly backward through time at lightning speed, illuminating your identity down past your parents and grandparents, past the countless generations before them, your ancestors roaming from continent to continent, your primate ancestors, down through all the animals that preceded them, back through the earliest life, into the first living cell, then plunging down into the complex chemicals that made it possible, down into the molten planet and the forming solar system, back to the birth of your carbon and oxygen and iron atoms in a thousand different stars exploding across the galaxy, back through the evolution of the visible galaxy itself deep inside a giant halo of dark matter, back through the universal expansion to the creation of your elementary particles—that you are made of at this very moment—in the Big Bang.

This is science. And yet it is also a prayer—to align ourselves with the universe so that each of us can experience who we are. Who we are depends on our history. How far back we understand that history—how much of our own identity we claim—is up to us. No earlier generation could even have imagined the scale of our true identity.

On a clear and moonless night, go far from electric lights, let your eyes slowly become adapted to the dark, and contemplate the Milky Way. Using your disciplined imagination, don't be satisfied with seeing a glowing whitish streak across the dome of the sky, the way the ancients did (that's why they called it the Royal Road, the Milky Way, the heavenly Nile). Let your knowledge of the galaxy deepen what you see, and it will expand what you are. Look *through* the Milky Way into its third dimension. Take some time. Suddenly everything will shift and you'll realize you're seeing an immense spiral galaxy *edge-on*—and you are inside the disk.

The galaxy is merely our local geography. There is a whole universe to re-envision, large and small, outside and inside ourselves. Expanding our consciousness to the spiritual realms of the universe is praying.

Awakening to small-scale reality, as much as large-scale reality, can also be prayer. According to the neuroscientist Jill Bolte Taylor in her famous TED talk about recovering from a massive stroke, every morning she says to her fifty trillion cells, "Thank you, girls, for another great day!" It took the aspirations and work of countless generations to achieve this kind of knowledge, but that's what lets her experience gratitude on this profound level.

Peace of mind flows from living in a sane, coherent, and meaningful big picture of ourselves and our place in the universe. When we find that place, that's God answering our prayers, metaphorically saying, "This is who you humans are and what you can be. Let me open your eyes to this."

Who would not love this? Does it love us? I think we can say yes, God loves us, even though God doesn't feel it. The emerging God doesn't have feelings for me the way I might have feelings for it, but its *effects* can be like those of a person who did feel love for me: it gives me endless gifts, it supports me in my weakness, it never deserts me, it encourages me and inspires new ideas, and it asks only that I recognize our relationship. If that isn't love, what is it? From a larger viewpoint the very idea of love depends on having a complicated emerging God. A pure feeling of attachment to another is something that many animals seem to have, with some even forming lifelong bonds, but to seek and treasure that feeling and call it love takes aspirations. It takes meaning. It takes God. God may or may not love us, depending on how you look at it, but God is what makes it possible for us to love one another.

We have a role to play on every size scale along the Uroboros of Human Identity, and we can experience all of them and begin to understand how we fit into God and how God fits into the universe. This is an opportunity with enormous ramifications. It could be humanity's saving grace. A real God needs us to pay attention to reality.

Praying can be a way to discover those root aspirations at the core of us, the aspirations that don't shift with the external pressures and tastes of the moment. It's a way to stay in contact with them, to live on their level. Until I knew mine, I had no connection to God.

When my aspiration was just to lose weight, nothing happened, but when it became working the twelve steps and finding a new and coherent perspective on my life, everything happened. Root aspirations are what make a prayer sincere. Otherwise we're praying for what we may not want or even understand but think we should. Maybe *pray* is not the only word for what I am describing, but it definitely involves a spiritual conversation. It's not my lower self begging my higher self for something, as I once thought; it's putting myself imaginatively in a more cosmic way of thinking and talking to bring my actions into accord. It's a kind of spiritual balancing act.

So, yes, God answers prayers, and yet no being is out there listening.

For me it has been a joy to know that God is real and that spiritual language does not have to be fluff. With modern cosmology we've come into the equivalent of a fabulous inheritance that could change everything for generations to come. It's providing a new kind of symbolism, and symbolism is the medium of spirituality. If we use our god-capacity together with our best knowledge, we have the possibility of transcending our confused and conflicting symbols of God.

If we can express in an emotionally resonant way the process of God's emerging and the titanic force it has become on planet Earth; if we appreciate how wondrously the emerging God welcomes us into the cosmos; if we grasp that this collective phenomenon of God creates the meaning of our cosmic context; if we put ourselves into this reality by praying, meditating, visualizing, and participating, we'll begin to think cosmically. We'll find untapped strength and wisdom and the willingness to deal with whatever is before us. This is my candidate for the highest and best use of our god-capacity. Will we give it a chance?

Once we understand what God is, we can stop thinking about it. After all, the more we think about identifying God, the more objectively we have to look at it and the more distant that makes us feel from it—which defeats the purpose of drawing strength from closeness. Once the question of God's existence is taken off the table, we can breathe more easily, talk to God, and understand what we're doing.

I don't remember this stuff all the time. I slide into default triviality like anyone else. But if I notice I'm doing that, I can throw open the doors again to the spiritual size scales of my consciousness and my universe and inhale God. Every deep personal change has a quiet element of maintenance. There's no magic to it. It's a discipline. Try to hold the doors open. Because life is majestic if you can hold a cosmic perspective. Pray, pray, pray.

CHAPTER 6

Is There an Afterlife?

In many religious traditions the afterlife is when we get to see God or be with Him or understand the mysteries that made no sense and had to be accepted on faith while we were alive. The afterlife may be seen as a reward or a punishment or sometimes simply the next stage in the ongoing story of ourselves. But once we start thinking about God not as a separate being but as a complex and marvelous phenomenon emerging from the interacting aspirations of our species in the scientifically known universe, the afterlife takes on a far more encompassing meaning.

No matter what anyone claims, it's impossible to imagine our own consciousness completely extinguished, because we have to use that consciousness to imagine it. This doesn't mean our consciousness can't be extinguished, but since we can't imagine that happening, it feels intuitively impossible and thus primes us to wonder about an afterlife.

Just as we humans have a god-capacity, we have what we might call an afterlife-capacity. The afterlife-capacity is the ability to focus on the possibility of an afterlife, to try to understand how it might work, and to prepare ourselves and our loved ones for it. Archeologists have uncovered ancient burial sites throughout the world in which bodies were accompanied by objects that might be of use in some future existence. Given the importance of the afterlife to our species, let me ask the question parallel to the one I asked about our god-capacity in chapter 5: At this moment in history, what is the highest and best use of our afterlife-capacity? By *best* I again mean best for both the individual and the planet upon which our lives and all our purposes depend.

We all want to be part of something meaningful that's larger than ourselves. It's a hunger, the hunger to belong to, and participate in, some purpose that validates our existence. This hunger must be satisfied—but our challenge is to do so in the real universe. What we need is a way to think productively about the afterlife *now*. While we can't know directly what's going to happen after we die, we do know that how we think about the afterlife affects our lives right now—and this isn't just idle speculation. The afterlife-capacity is a *capacity*: If it's used well, it can change our lives for the better. But it can also be misused to foster resignation or fear or to control others.

There was a big controversy in my town a few years ago about a mural that a boy painted on a school wall. Some angry parents claimed it "looked like heaven"—as though heaven were a city and they knew what it looked like. The concepts of heaven and hell can still be useful but not if they're taken literally. "Heaven" is an aspiration. Looking forward to heaven has helped many people get through hard times. Hell, on the other hand, may sound like an alternative to heaven, but it's not. Hell has nothing to do with aspirations. It's a form of social control, not for the guilty but for the innocent. The promise of hell for the hated makes the innocent injured feel avenged and perhaps less likely to take matters into their own hands; the possibility of hell for the innocent if they transgress keeps those poor people in line, since eternity is too long to risk. People invent many versions of heaven for themselves, but no one would ever invent the idea of hell for themselves. They have to be carefully taught to believe in hell.

Not long ago I attended a fabulous mixed-media dance performance by Tandy Beal that artistically explored the idea of the afterlife. I was particularly struck by a series of brief video interviews scattered throughout the show in which a random assortment of people, including children, described what they thought would happen to them after they die. They presented a wide range of notions, from the old-fashioned heaven with harps and angels to being spirited away to bizarre alien worlds. Some expected reincarnation on Earth and were surprisingly certain about even small details, while others dismissed the whole idea of the afterlife as wishful thinking. No one, incidentally, saw a future in hell. But all of them, without exception, answered as *isolated beings* and saw their afterlife fate, whatever it might be or not be, as theirs personally.

But you can't see the real afterlife from a me-alone viewpoint.

We tend to see ourselves as a flower on a tree, and when we fall off, our overwhelming concern is what happens to our petals. But as the only beings with our kind of consciousness in the known universe, we have a much bigger role. We are the consciousness not only of the flower but of the tree, the roots, the DNA, the seeds just eaten by a bird and being carried at this moment to an unknown destination. We are the only consciousness of the pollen on the bee, the fertilized flower on a distant tree that the bee later visits, and the new trees that grow from the seeds. We are the consciousness of the entire planet, coming to terms with life as a four-billion-year-old force, permeating its every crevice, surface, and body of water. Coming to see ourselves as we cosmically are is a revelation of our immense and lasting value to the universe and of our larger meaning, which we can't even glimpse with a me-alone sense of the afterlife.

When our ancestors mentally lived in small universes, the ideas of heaven or reincarnation may have exhausted their afterlife-capacity, but focusing our precious afterlife-capacity on these ideas today can never inspire us to become our full selves in *this* life in *this* universe or in the future that is actually coming. It will never let us participate in the universe we actually live in or appreciate what we actually are.

We can discover a huge afterlife for all of us as soon as we stop thinking of ourselves as nothing but a me-alone consciousness.

Science doesn't rule out an afterlife, but a few numbers might encourage us to take a bigger perspective. The probability that any one of us would have come into existence even once is so vanishingly small that our current consciousness could be seen as a miracle. The probability that our very same consciousness would come into existence again is virtually nil. During your mother's reproductive lifetime, she had maybe three hundred eggs that matured and could have become fertilized. Your father, on the other hand, produced on the order of a hundred million sperm per ejaculation, not per lifetime. So just between your parents, there were *hundreds of billions* of possible children they could have produced, but only *you*, and maybe a handful of siblings, got the chance. To really get this, meditate on an empty chair. The number of brothers and sisters that your parents could have conceived—who might have sat in that chair but never will—could have filled planets. The same minuscule probability existed that either of your parents would be born, not to mention the minute probability that they would find each other at the right time. Multiply these fractional probabilities by each other all the way back, fractions of fractions of fractions, past all your human ancestors, past all your animal ancestors, to the awakening of the first living cell on Earth, and you've never seen such a tiny number. The probability was nanosmall for any one of us—yet we made it. We are the grand prize winners in the cosmic lottery. Gratitude is called for. To ask for a second shot for an identical consciousness completely misses the point of how extraordinarily improbable we were in the first place.

Scientific cosmology has made it clear that the universe is materially and structurally far different from earlier imaginings of it. The corollary is this: so are we. We're not just skin-sealed packages of organs and bones animated by a soul. Nor are we, as the mythologist Joseph Campbell once suggested, "scum on the face of an average planet of an average star." We humans, when viewed from a cosmic perspective, are something extraordinary, but unless we take that cosmic perspective, our extraordinariness is not even visible.

There's no point in speculating on what happens to us after death until we understand what we are before death. The real question is, *What are we while we're alive?* Our first job is to find out what we are—not just *who* we are, our personal identity, but *what* we are, the primal identity we all share. Because this identity will play an outsized role in our afterlife.

Every one of us has the entire history of the universe built into us on multiple size scales. The hydrogen atoms in the water in our bodies at this very moment came straight out of the Big Bang. The rest of our atoms may have originated millions or billions of years ago in exploding supernovas far across the galaxy. We share with animals cells and organs that have barely changed for millions of years, and our brains are the same brains our early Cro-Magnon ancestors had when they first painted with artistry on the walls of their caves. Each of us *is* the human race where we stand—in fact, we are what the Big Bang itself is doing right now, where we stand. We are not just individuals—and that's not a matter of choice but a fact, whether we recognize it or not. Escaping the me-alone mentality is a revelation.

Ecclesiastes, in the provocative translation by Rami Shapiro, says, "All is impermanence": in the end we are ashes to ashes, dust to dust, whether we were good or bad, wise or stupid. This may be true *on the individual scale* but not in the larger picture. According to Ecclesiastes, the world was unchanging, and there was "nothing new under the sun." The long timescales we are aware of today, and the changes that have occurred during them—protohumans' becoming extinct, the evolution of life, and the expansion of the universe—were simply unimaginable to Ecclesiastes. But not to us.

Arguably the most important person in the history of the world was mitochondrial Eve, who lived in Africa more than 100,000 years ago. Humanity passed through a desperate bottleneck at some point, and the only survivors were her descendants. We know this because today all humans share the mitochondria of her cells, with of course a few local mutations. These few show us how little we have diverged from each other since then. Mitochondrial Eve could never have imagined that she would be the ancestral matriarch of *all* future humans and that the distant descendants of all the other women she knew of would die out. Her brain would not have been capable of such a thought, even if she was the most intelligent being of her time. Nevertheless she founded the human race as we know it. Is this impermanence? On Ecclesiastes's scale, yes, because Eve died like everyone else. But on the scale of human evolution, she far outshines Alexander the Great, Jesus, Shakespeare, or anyone you can name.

We are not just me-alone individuals.

Here's another way of thinking about this. We're social animals. Our lives continually intersect with one another's. Some scientists insist that the mind and the brain are one and the same, but those who say that mind is something shared with others are more convincing to me. If I'm talking to you, you are in my mind, and I'm in yours—though our brains are not inside each other. If the mind is something larger than any single person and transcends any single person, then it might continue to have effects after the person is dead, not by any magical means but by living on in other people's minds. "Living on" in this sense: sometimes when a person close to you has died and you're facing some big decision, you imagine asking them what you should do, and you hear their answer, not yours, and you realize that's what they *would have* said. But where did that answer come from? You never discussed this topic with them. There is something more than memories still living in your mind, because you can somehow reconstruct another mind's thought process so that it can still inspire surprising insights.

Some evolutionary biologists wonder why people help strangers, especially in faraway countries, since this appears to be a suicidal waste of resources from the point of view of perpetuating our genes. These evolutionary biologists suggest that this kind of altruism might be merely a costly by-product of an important trait like em-pathy. But perpetuation of your own genes is the highest goal only if you are an isolated package of organs. If you are the human species, and you are beginning to experience yourself as such, then contrib-uting to foreigners under many circumstances makes perfect sense. It perpetuates our larger identity.

We are part of each other, not just part of God. It may be that our minds permeate others' minds like halos of dark matter, invisible but attracted gravitationally, changing shapes as their gravitational fields endlessly interact. How crazy it would be to think of dark mat-ter as nothing but a lot of particles when collectively it creates and controls the galaxies. Newness emerges collectively.

It's easy to assume that humanity means "all the people on Earth," but this completely ignores our time dimension. Humanity is not just a group of people: it's human evolution on planet Earth. Humanity is the great biological and cultural crescendo from early hominids to the majesty and horror of the prolific yet perhaps en-dangered species that we are at this moment and on into the largely undetermined future. We are not just individuals, because we are inescapably part of that emerging reality.

This perspective opens the door to a meaningful afterlife.

CONSCIOUSNESS

Twice I have sat on panels at public events that were exploring views of the afterlife. I heard many people's questions, both to me and to the other panelists, and could not help noticing that when people ponder what will happen to them after death, what they really want to know is what will happen to their consciousness. It seems most of us are not much interested in what will happen to our atoms af-ter death, though that is actually fascinating and something we can knowledgeably discuss. No, the burning question is whether the consciousness *that each of us currently identifies as "me"* will somehow continue after we die.

What is that consciousness that we're thinking might continue? Is it our tastes and personality? Is it our memories? Is it the silent witness? Does all of it have to continue or maybe just a few whispers?

Scientifically no one knows yet what an individual consciousness is, even though we all experience it. There is a Hindu tradition that consciousness existed before anything else and created the material world; in this understanding, which still has its scientific as well as religious partisans today, we humans are more like receivers of this universal consciousness than transmitters. But this idea seems to me to have become much less probable since the dark matter–dark energy recipe for the universe was discovered.

Consciousness can't be spread vaguely throughout the universe, because, as you'll recall, dark matter, dark energy, and clouds of hydrogen and helium gas—99.99 percent of the contents of our universe—cannot be conscious. They're too simple to think. Something existed 13.8 billion years ago, out of which our galaxy and planet evolved, but it was not "conscious" until consciousness emerged in some creature on some world. Consciousness can include everything from the minimal awareness of a single-celled creature that is bumping its way through a water droplet on a leaf all the way up to the self-consciousness of the universe. But no matter what level of consciousness you're talking about, consciousness as we know it (it's useless to talk about consciousness as we don't know it) can emerge only in regions of highly concentrated stardust. Only stardust can engage in the required exponentially complicating interactions—as it has for the past 4.5 billion years on planet Earth, spawning layer upon layer of emergent phenomena. Until self-consciousness emerged in evolution, there was simply no meaning whatsoever to anything nor was there anyone who might be bothered by this.

Consciousness is an emergent phenomenon. Like all emergent phenomena, including God, it is qualitatively different from its constituent cells yet made up of them and dependent on their endless interactions. Consciousness is not free floating. It's continually effervescing from us complex stardust creatures. It can't exist independent of us, not even for an instant. Indefinitely keeping a consciousness alive but disembodied, whether in heaven for eternity or temporarily in storage for the right rebirth opportunity, would be an insuperable difficulty. Some technology worshippers are confident that a medium can be devised to preserve the information that creates a consciousness. But there is no way to test if they're right, because even if they succeed in preserving something, there will be no way to know if the stored consciousness is the consciousness in question, except to be it.

IMMORTALITY

Although preserving an individual consciousness would be a problem, there is a scientific-sounding afterlife theory being championed today by several well-regarded scientists and described in popular books. It's a modern version of immortality, set in the "superuniverse" or "multiverse." That's the realm theoretically outside our universe—not just outside our visible patch of universe but outside the whole universe created by the Big Bang. This version of immortality is based on a theory called *eternal inflation*, which I discussed in chapter 3. (Unlike the double dark theory, which is supported by overwhelming evidence, there is zero evidence yet for eternal inflation, just mathematical beauty.)

Eternal inflation posits that there are two states of being: spacetime and inflation. Spacetime is what we're familiar with inside our universe. But outside our Big Bang is an endless realm of inflation. The idea of inflation is that in any tiny unit of time every region doubles in size, and in the next equal unit it doubles again, on and on, unbound by and quickly surpassing the speed of light. In eternal inflation space is exploding so fast that no two regions can ever come together to form anything, not even an atom, so nothing can ever evolve. If this state of being exists, it must continue forever—but even the most unlikely things happen eventually, so by the laws of probability tiny pockets, or bubbles, form in it and slow down instead of speeding up. These bubbles are big bangs. They may evolve into other universes with laws of physics different from ours, hence the name for the whole shebang is the multiverse.

So here's the afterlife connection: if the multiverse is *literally infinite*, then theoretically in all those bubble universes there could be not just one or a hundred rebirths of your identical consciousness but an infinite number, popping up here and there for all eternity. Breathtaking immortality! At first. But then you realize that even if the theory is correct—a big if—those other yous are in other universes. They will never be discoverable or in contact with your consciousness, so there's no afterlife *for you* in hypothesizing them.

This search for personal immortality has gone on since the birth of civilization.

"The Epic of Gilgamesh" is one of humanity's oldest preserved stories, ancient already in the ancient world, a story of a Sumerian king and his failed quest for immortality. The only human beings that get to be immortal, Gilgamesh discovers, are the old couple who built a boat and survived the great flood that the gods sent to destroy the world. This was the prototype for the Noah story. Not humans but archetypes like Noah become immortal in our world. Ironically Gilgamesh's failure to achieve immortality was so archetypal that he too has achieved immortality. But it's literary immortality, not literal.

Immortality for many people today no longer means living forever but rather that after they die everyone will remember *their name*. Their name will have the afterlife, not their consciousness. The loser who shot John Lennon did it for this kind of immortality. I intentionally don't remember his name. But we are much more likely to achieve a meaningful immortality if future people don't simply recall our names but are actually changed and helped by what we have done and as a result are more able to carry on this great experiment of intelligence evolving and God emerging. How can we achieve this?

We can look at consciousness collectively. No one fully understands what an individual consciousness is, but it's sometimes easier to understand the broad sweep than the individual details. This has certainly been true for the dark matter search. The collective nature of dark matter has been understood for decades and has changed our whole picture of the universe, even though as of this writing no one yet knows what the particle is. We can say with assurance that, collectively, consciousness is the crown jewel of the universe, without which nothing else would matter. This collective aspect of us, not our individual consciousnesses, can become immortal—but it's our individual consciousnesses that encompass our role in the collective consciousness.

Nothing and no one can be literally immortal now. But something can have characteristics now that give it the *chance* of immortality, and that's what we humans have, if we define *immortal* as "so long as human intelligence continues." If there is no human intelligence, there will be no human ideas like immortality. If we play our cards right, we can become immortal beyond all religions' wildest dreams, though whether we *will* play our cards right is not determined yet. It can happen only if we understand what we are on all size scales—and *act accordingly*.

So whether we become immortal is actually up to us.

CONSCIOUSNESS ON THE LARGE SCALE

Each of us *is* the process of human evolution *as it is happening today where we stand*. We are the representatives of our entire species, past and future, to twenty-first-century Earth. We who are alive today are the hands of our ancestors and descendants. Their chances depend on us. Through us humans Earth is becoming self-aware, and so we must, for Earth's sake, see humanity as Earth does, collectively, across millions of years. We may be the beginning of something huge that is developing in this universe, carried out through the long-distance multigenerational pioneering of space. We could be the beginning of intelligence in our galaxy. What if we are?

What if *assuming* we are the beginning of intelligence in our galaxy is what makes it possible? One of my favorite cartoons shows a guy jumping up in protest at the climate change summit, yelling, "What if it's all a hoax and we create a better world for nothing?" What if we humans decide to live up to the standard of being the beginning of intelligence in the visible universe, and it turns out we're not the beginning of intelligence but just part of it? Will it all have been for nothing? We'll be here to find out. What could be better than that?

Our role as the self-consciousness of the planet can grow indefinitely—and we blessed jackpot winners have an obligation to our ancestors and descendants to do everything we can to make sure it does indeed grow. But that's not all. We have an obligation to be the self-consciousness of the universe. Only the universe's self-consciousness, which understands the enormous length of time and the mind-boggling number of improbabilities that were overcome to evolve us, can understand what the universe has already invested in us. Only the self-consciousness of the universe can understand how important it is to protect self-consciousness. Intelligence is something bigger than Earth. In some sense Earth may have to put up with us humans. But we should make it as easy for Earth as we can.

Our consciousness, when in the service of our planet and universe, knows it's not just the petals of the flower. We self-conscious intelligent beings have a cosmic role. It's big. It's wonderful. And when we think about the afterlife, the immortality of *this* big self is what we should be caring about.

Through us, as well as through intelligent aliens, if they exist, the universe has evolved far beyond the single-celled kind of consciousness. The universe recognizes that it has a unified self with a name we conscious beings have given it. And how is the universe doing this? It's using its brain. Us. We in the cosmic club of intelligent beings—and it may be a very small club—are the self-consciousness of the universe. We are the brain cells of the cosmos. To the extent that we become conscious of the universe, the universe becomes conscious of itself.

Given how little stardust there is, islands of consciousness must be extremely rare. These islands are the universe's only chance to reflect on or appreciate itself, its contents, and the details of its unlikely but awe-inspiring story. The importance of each island of consciousness *to the universe* (i.e., not just to ourselves) is vastly disproportionate to our size.

Or so we cosmic islands can see it.

BECOMING AN ANCESTOR

There's one thing we actually *know* happens to us after life: we become ancestors. Many cultures greatly esteem ancestors. Blind deference to ancestors is paralysis for a culture, but practicing esteem and gratitude toward ancestors is good for us, because it gives us a sense of continuity and an appreciation of what it took to make us. Without a sense of continuity and how it extends into the future as well as the past, we can't understand the consequences of our actions. Considering the thousands of years of future consequences that modern technologies have already unleashed, understanding them now could make all the difference.

Thinking about ourselves as ancestors can illuminate the meaning of both our lives right now and the afterlife. I want to enjoy the position of esteemed ancestor while I'm alive. So I have to try to figure out what will make me an esteemed ancestor and do it.

Today may seem ordinary to us, but it will be mythic in the future of our planet, because it is a pivotal moment. This is the end of more than two centuries in which both the human population and the amount of resources consumed per person expanded exponentially. For the rest of the world population to reach the standard of living of the First World would take the resources of four Earths. We don't have them. It's not a political statement but simply math that tells us this trend must change fairly soon. The fate of countless human generations (not to mention millions of species) is riding on what we who are alive now decide to do while humanity still has the resources and ability to solve global problems.

So to me the central moral question of our time is, What are we ancestors supposed to be doing *now* to contribute to human success on a cosmological timescale? This question should be asked before every law is passed. It should be asked during every budgetary review. *What should worthy ancestors be doing now?* We may not be our brother's keeper, but we are our great-great-grandchildren's keeper. And so is our brother. On this, if nothing else, we ought to be able to agree.

Those great-great-grandchildren are a lot more valuable to us right now than our actions would suggest. Economics tells us to discount the present value of any good that won't appear, or event that won't occur, for a long time. Misapplying this formula to human beings, we discount the value of their lives, treating people of the future like some kind of low-probability event, barely worth worrying about. But what is inevitable is real. The future exists. It just hasn't happened yet. *Our connection to it exists now*, even if we don't know exactly what it is. In fact, the value of almost everything we do or create, from raising a family to writing a book to starting a company, depends on that connection. If the connection were broken—if we knew, instead, that we would have a normal life but shortly after we die the human race would go extinct—for most people everything but short-term pleasure would lose its purpose. *We* need those future people *now*. To them we owe a spiritual debt for making our lives worthwhile.

The payback for being an honored ancestor is *now*. Our lives take flight. This is spirituality to me. Spirituality, as I defined it earlier, is about *experiencing my connection to what I believe exists*—and that includes not only God and the universe but the future.

We might become ancestors that those descendants will honor, and if we seriously try to figure out what that requires of us now, and we do it the best we can, then we can enjoy the spiritual high of being esteemed ancestors *now*. We can claim this identity now—but only if we learn how to think about the universe as it really is and take the long view. We could be seen from the future as a godlike race that turned the destruction of Earth around, just as the Egyptians of 1500 BCE believed a godlike race had built the pyramids a thousand years earlier and set their high civilization on its course.

If we enlarge our outlook and treasure our collective afterlife now while we're alive, the results will certainly benefit the humans of the future. But we don't even need to do it for them. We should do it for ourselves. Every time I help another addict, I'm helping myself, because *recovery is a collective event*. Humanity too is a collective event. When we aim to benefit our descendants as far into the future as possible, we ourselves benefit *immediately* by becoming large-minded people aware of their power. This awareness can energize our days, deepen our social bonds, and inspire creativity in whatever kind of work we do. Aiming to help the future is the best thing we can do for ourselves right now.

We humans are part of an immense blossoming of consciousness that has burst beyond itself and ignited as God, and it may be happening only here, on planet Earth. We need to take care of our planet. We live forever *only* if this astonishing evolutionary achievement of the universe—intelligent, self-reflecting, and aspiring life—continues. This is how I interpret the biblical imperative "Choose life!" Every action we take to increase the probability of survival, happiness, justice, and health for our species and planet is an investment in our own immortality.

As long as our aspiring species lives on, so will God—and so will every one of our aspirations, because they are all part of God. Consequently God's self-interest is in keeping humanity going, and I see this as a major advantage for us.

The way to immortality is to *identify with what is immortal*, or at the least very long-lived, and that is our species, intelligence, our galaxy, and cosmos. It isn't that hard to do. As the Uroboros of

Human Identity illustrates, people's sense of identity has drastically expanded over history, from members of a family and tribe to members of an industry, country, or world religion. It's time to take the next step. But not a half-step, a giant leap.

After death there's plenty of time for us collectively, just not individually. We fit into something huge, literally cosmic, and we don't have to be alive to stay part of it.

We don't have to corset our afterlife-capacity in old-fashioned imagery or else throw it away. An eternal heaven, reincarnation, or simple extinction of the individual at death all seem pretty paltry sources of meaning compared to what's available in this universe. From a cosmic perspective, heaven is here. We're living in it right now. It looks like every photograph ever taken, the suffering as well as the joy. It looks like Midgard. Heaven is the *opposite* of eternally unchanging perfection: it is infinite potential with lots of time to evolve—an invaluable gift from a universe that does not bestow it lightly and then only on the luckiest stardust oases. We don't have to do anything to make this planet heaven—just stop making it hell.

And take a cosmic perspective. If we're the beginning of intelligence in the galaxy, we could also be the beginning of intelligence in the entire visible universe, since in the distant future our galaxy (by then Milky Andromeda) will *be* the visible universe. If that actually happens, then God will have become universal—but not before.

We humans can go on forever, seeding the entire future visible universe with *the kind of intelligence that generates God*. But this will happen only if every generation invests in the long-range interests of the generations that follow. This gets my vote for the highest and best use of our afterlife-capacity.

PART III

CHAPTER 7

Renewing God, Renewing Religion

Are you wondering what will happen to your religion if you reconsider your image of God? Will it lose its center? Will it fall apart?

No, but your religion will change for you. For the better.

Our religions can be as important to us today as they have ever been to anyone in history but only if they support us in integrating our way of thinking about God into a positive, coherent, accurate worldview. The scientific picture is not optional. No one would hire an engineer, an architect, or a pilot who thought gravity was an optional consideration. We are building a bridge to a God that is real—that can empower us both intellectually and spiritually through the real and momentous challenges of the coming decades and centuries. Let's start with the strongest foundation possible. We live in an age that has seen enormous progress not only in the sciences and technology but in human rights and global awareness, yet none of this progress has been truly integrated into the teachings of any major religion. Religions, values, and mythic stories are still the form that best embodies meaning for us, but we need that meaning to help import the real picture into our hearts and imaginations.

Shakespeare is still performed because his plays still speak to us, only we interpret them differently today. To appreciate the human understanding, delight, emotion, and verbal inventiveness of the plays, we don't have to believe in absolute monarchy or think that fathers should wield absolute power over their daughters' mate choice, even though these were assumptions of Shakespeare's time. Instead we ask what the plays say about *our* character and *our* times. Those who love their scriptures should be asking these same questions: Why here? Why now? This is how to honor our sacred literature: by reinterpreting and reimagining it anew for every age. In fact, this is what *keeps* literature sacred. Once it no longer speaks to the present, it has fossilized.

If we want our scriptures and religions to live and speak to our time, we can take at least four actions to bring them into harmony with reality and in this way transform our spiritual worldview into a source of strength and wisdom for a planet in transition. It's impossible to renew a religion by tinkering around the edges, but a commitment to do these four daring things will make all the difference:

1. Break the spiritual glass ceiling.
2. Reject literalism.
3. Find the "truth box."
4. Honor what is sacred to *everyone*.

BREAK THE SPIRITUAL GLASS CEILING

The job of prophets has always been to call into question the assumptions of their society and teach a deeper moral truth. But beneath all assumptions about us humans lie thousands of unspoken assumptions about our *physical* world. No one questions whether the earth will remain beneath our feet tomorrow. Our life experience makes that perfectly clear. But beyond Earth we rely on equations, metaphors, and hearsay. We are in the land of assumptions. If we presume to talk about the universe and God without ever questioning these assumptions, we have nowhere to go spiritually but along well-beaten paths. How many people lately have outdone Moses, Buddha, Jesus, Lao-tzu, and the other great teachers who lived thousands of years ago? What progress has been made—not in

intellectual notions of theology but in the arising of more enlight-
ened or cosmically conscious human beings?

Individuals can make great spiritual progress in their lifetime, yet
they don't surpass the great masters of the past.

Why?

The reason is simple: without science we are permanently trapped
beneath a spiritual glass ceiling. We can never rise higher, no matter
how good, moral, brilliant, and wise we may be, because there is a
limit to what earthbound metaphors can communicate. No matter
how poetic and loving the great spiritual leaders may have been, no
matter how deeply they experienced their heaven and earth, they
never experienced *the slightest* connection to the universe we actually live in. They thought we lived on a flat earth with a domed sky
where favored people could walk on water. We don't live in that
universe. Many of their teachings may be timelessly invaluable, but
they're incomplete: they can't tell us how to relate to our universe or
how to bring our behavior and our technologies into harmony with
it on size scales or timescales they didn't even know existed.

The great teachers could not have conceived of a scientifically
real God nor even of the need for one.

The modern world needs to see beyond the worldview of those
religious figures to free the next person with the rare human and
spiritual capabilities of Jesus or Buddha to experience the new universe and speak to the future world. We don't have to be as good
as Jesus to see beyond his worldview in many respects. We have
all the tools; we need to use them, and time is of the essence. The
climate of Earth is transitioning, weather events are becoming more
extreme, the oceans are rising, and forests are dying. When refu-
gees from deluged islands and coastal cities worldwide are fighting for territory just to live on; when once-tropical diseases spread
unchecked; when people panic and become violent because without
a shared vision they don't know what to do, how is that future Jesus or Buddha supposed to inspire a frightened, fragmented world
using only baggage-burdened metaphors from a tiny prescientific

universe? Goodness plus charisma will not be enough without a new vision that's equally true for everyone on Earth and can be expressed in inspiring and inclusive metaphors. *The goodness standard needs a conceptual ladder to climb.*

The spiritual glass ceiling can be shattered by science—but science alone can't give anyone the strength to climb through the opening or the compassion and wisdom to know what to do when they get there. And yet inevitably, once the opening is there, aspiring young people will appear who can climb beyond.

REJECT LITERALISM

Humans have the extraordinary ability, unique as far as we know, to create new ideas by combining and recombining imagery and concepts in infinite variations, endlessly inspiring and entertaining each other. This could never happen if we took all words literally, because then mentally we would be trapped in the material world that our eyes can see. The power to use metaphor, to turn a solid idea liquid, is a huge part of human intelligence. All religions are based on this ability, yet many modern believers miss the point and try to freeze the meaning of words into chunks of ice.

Literalism is a step backward in cognitive evolution; it's a willful abandonment of the ability to think metaphorically—to let language transport the imagination and create endless newness. Literalism is a loss of brain connections or perhaps a resistance to making them—for fear, for power, for oppression. It's a giving up on life's potential and a shortsighted way to seek spiritual comfort. Consider, for example, the enormous damage done to America's public schools by armies of literalists organizing to prevent children, not only their own, from learning anything that might challenge a literal reading of Genesis—and in doing so, battling more and more areas of science. When the National Air and Space Museum in Washington, DC, made *Cosmic Voyage*, the first IMAX movie about cosmology and evolution, the museum's administrator tried at first to get the filmmaker to portray the origin of the universe without using the term *Big Bang*. The administrator feared a boycott of the museum by scriptural literalists. Fortunately the filmmaker's scientist advisors refused to go along, and the Big Bang was restored. The boycotts never happened.

Literalism in religion is not a legitimate philosophical or spiritual choice. It's a kind of illness. Almost any religion can be a guide to a loving purposeful life if its teachings are subordinated to human compassion and scientifically supported reality. But taking its narratives literally requires giving the mundane priority over the cosmic and rectitude priority over compassion. Dogma taken literally can lead to violent and even insane behavior.

One of the most extreme literalist ideas in circulation in the United States today is supposedly based on biblical prophecy: the world cannot be saved—so politically there is no point in trying. These Christian literalists believe the second coming of Jesus will begin with the Rapture, when true believers will be physically lifted to heaven, where they'll never have to deal with science because there won't be any physical bodies or any real world to enforce physical laws. But according to the history of religion scholar Elaine Pagels, visions of end times were actually a political metaphor; the Revelation to John was predicting the destruction of Rome by angelic armies and the salvation of the faithful, who would be rewarded. In every era since, the Revelation to John has been interpreted as predicting the fall of *whatever* political power was considered evil at the time. Literalists misinterpret its meaning by ignoring the historical context of the writing.

The Bible nowhere praises ignorance. The people who wrote it offered the truest story of their time, but their words—which were often metaphorical even to them—cannot be taken literally as the story of *our* time. And in fact they're not: literalists always cherry-pick. Do today's biblical literalists refuse to drive cars and demand chariots because Ezekiel saw a flaming chariot? The cars, planes, and computers they conveniently use are based on the same scientific principles as the cosmology of the expanding universe. If you don't require a chariot, you don't require a young Earth or an apocalypse to escape from profound confusion. We owe better to our children.

The unselfishness, energy, and spirit of so many good people have been misdirected into battling scientific truth as the enemy simply because it is inconsistent with their literal reading of scripture. This misdirection might once have been honest, but now that we know better, maintaining the pretense is not. It's immoral.

The worship of literalism is the love of words over the Word.

True, literalism is not new. In the Middle Ages scholars considered scripture true *by definition*. But before equating the medieval version of literalism with the modern one, consider this. At least those scholars did not believe that *only* the scriptures were true. The "authority of the ancients" was the medieval standard of truth. There were competing writings from many ancient pagan sources—particularly the Greeks and Romans—that demanded enough respect that serious effort was put into reconciling them with scripture. Maybe those today who choose to believe that their preferred religious scripture is literally true should, like their medieval forebears, be required to believe that the writings of the nonbelievers are also true. Half of medieval thinking has been adopted by today's combative scriptural literalists of all types, but the essential other half has been conveniently forgotten. And with it has disappeared all humility.

Once we reject literalism, we can *take back spiritual language*.

Spiritual language is an essential human tool. We need it to help evoke a feeling of connection to the universe—otherwise we'll never feel the universe matters to us or we to it. If we don't feel those things, we won't bother to understand it, and thus we'll never be coherent intellectually, emotionally, and cosmically. Spiritual language helps give reality meaning: It can make reality matter. It puts us viscerally into the big picture. Who is going to save a world that doesn't matter?

Science doesn't make sacred literature obsolete or even less than sacred. We just need to read it in light of our knowledge and our

times. If we tossed out all spiritual language, whether because religions have abused it or because we're attempting to be "scientific,"
our action would be as self-defeating as punishing children for getting low grades by not letting them go to school any more. We owe
religion a debt for so spectacularly developing the imagination in
our species, probably inspiring more art and storytelling than all the
rest of culture put together.

But now the rest of culture is changing quickly. We need to reinterpret the lasting core truths of our scriptures and other spiritual
writings in light of the world we live in today and the people we
hope to become. "Honor thy father and thy mother," for example,
has traditionally been a sacred duty, but only now are we realizing
that our true "father and mother" is the full sweep of our ancestors
back through the animal kingdom to the quarks and dark matter.
Honor all the way! We intelligent creatures have an awe-inspiring
parentage if we let the resonant words of our spiritual traditions
speak to our own universe.

But wait. Religious people are not the only literalists. Atheists
can also be guilty if they respond to the literal words used to describe God by people inevitably struggling for language and then
reject this straw man as being literally impossible. What does that
accomplish? They'll never convince believers to give up their beliefs. People never abandon deep spiritual assumptions simply because they're proved wrong but only if the assumption is *replaced by
a better idea*. Atheists may act in the best of faith, truly trying to save
believers from folly, but if they automatically label those people's
attempts to feel connected to the universe through spiritual metaphors as "belief in the supernatural," those atheists have missed the
point and helped no one.

It would be crazy to banish concepts like "God" or "blessing,"
invent arbitrary new words, and expect them to have any psychic
power. Who writes poetry in Esperanto? We can take back spiritual
language so long as we reinterpret the words to honor our universe

and the God of our species. By harmonizing our spiritual tools with our knowledge, we will deepen the resonance of those terms by orders of magnitude.

It will take artistry and study to harmonize our spiritual needs with the vast realms of scientific knowledge, both discovered and still to be explored. There's a lot of work to be done. But if we do it accurately and sensitively, thousands of newly refreshed words and phrases, no longer bogged down by tired religious connotations, can radiate like a galaxy and help light our way. "Blessings" don't come from a decision made by a single, all-powerful Will employing mysterious criteria to help some of us but not others. Blessings can be the insights and emotional gifts that shower us when we claim our place in the universe, accept its implications, especially for the nature of God, and try to live in harmony with the highest truth of our time.

We can take the glory of spiritual metaphor and shine it on reality.

FIND THE TRUTH BOX

Everything still in use needs to be cleaned out once in a while, and this is as true of religions as refrigerators. Bad or wrong ideas gradually smother a religion's essential messages in a million sticky notes tacked on by narrow-minded, power-oriented, or simply confused leaders. Those sticky notes need to be peeled off to unearth the lasting truths hidden beneath. There is no better time to do this than at the dawn of a new universe. But how do we go about this? It's not hard to clean a refrigerator, but how do you clean a religion?

There is a brilliant model we can use. It comes from science, which has a method of separating "best working knowledge" from those principles that we can confidently call truth. At first this may sound paradoxical, but it's quite profound: *No scientific theory can be both true and universally applicable.* In other words, you can never call a scientific theory true until you know its limits—where it stops being true, what it *can't* explain.

The clearest example is Newtonian physics, which is still taught to every physics student and still accurately describes how things fall when you drop them and how the planets orbit in our solar system. However, for any object traveling close to the speed of light or near the immense gravity of a black hole, Newton's laws don't apply, and you need Einstein's theory of relativity to calculate what's happening.

In the 1960s a philosopher of science named Thomas Kuhn wrote a book called *The Structure of Scientific Revolutions* that has misled generations into thinking that a new scientific theory, like Einstein's, simply overthrows the previous theory, in that case Newton's, and Newton's is no longer considered true. But Kuhn was wrong. Einstein's theory explains gravity in extreme circumstances, but in the ordinary circumstances we experience on Earth, the two theories make the same predictions.

Einstein's theory of relativity never *overthrew* Newtonian physics; it *enshrined* it. It drew a box around it—a truth box. *Inside* the box Newtonian physics can forever be considered true. This exalts Newtonian physics to what's actually the highest level of truth that exists in science: the truth of a theory whose limits we know. We can rely on it with absolute confidence—inside its truth box.

The idea of a truth box is a real humility enforcer. It prevents the kind of disastrous conflicts caused by competing religions, all claiming that their theories are both true *and* universal. *Only by defining the limits of a religion can you discover in what respects it is reliably true.* In the previous example, I should point out, no one has defined the truth box for relativity or quantum mechanics, so no one knows how far these theories can be trusted. They are our best working knowledge. Right now the best guess for a bigger theory that could encompass and define the limits of relativity and quantum mechanics is something called superstring theory, but so far there's zero evidence for it. Physicists are constantly trying to find the limits of their best theories, constantly forced to embrace their own humility in the process.

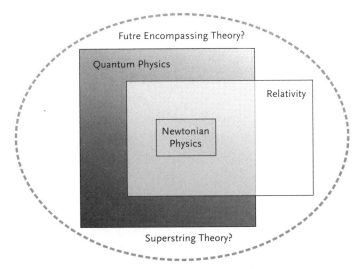

Figure 6. Truth boxes. Relativity and quantum physics both encompass Newtonian physics but not each other. They may in the future be encompassed in turn by superstring theory.

We can reinvigorate our religions and make them more inspirational and of greater service in the modern world by searching with rigorous honesty for the truth box of every religion and celebrating its contents with new and joyous rituals while accepting with humility that what lies outside the box (beloved as it may be) might not be true. Since all major religions were developed in prescientific times, their origin stories and pictures of physical, biological, and social reality reflect the thinking of those earlier times. The modern scientific picture can be to these religions as Einstein has been to Newton—that is, a later and better-supported theory that helps define the walls of the religion's truth box.

Science shows us that many scripturally based physical claims like the origin stories, if taken literally, lie far outside their religions' truth boxes and do not have the same truth status as the enduring core principles, such as "love your neighbor." Our spiritual challenge is to revisit traditional teachings to determine whether and how some can help us live in this new universe and motivate us to care for and protect each other and our planet. It is a spiritual challenge to find the limits of traditional teachings and create the next teachings. Far from tearing the center out of a religion, the emerging God illuminates it. God encompasses the truth box of every religion without threatening the religion's core truths.

If any religion today seriously attempts to find its truth box and reconcile with science, that religion will attract millions of grateful new adherents and find itself in a place of honor and influence in the emerging global civilization.

HONOR WHAT IS SACRED TO *EVERYONE*

I once heard a famous scientist say that the holy grail of science is to explain the universe without reference to God. That's a pretty ironic choice of metaphor. Without God there would be no concept of a holy grail. The bedrock belief of almost every scientist I have ever known is that truth is indeed the holy grail. Narrow or esoteric though their research specialty may seem to outsiders, when they make a discovery that they have worked toward for years and sometimes decades, they can experience what religious people might call the presence of divinity: a sense that they have pierced the veil of mystery and the universe has spoken directly to them in words never before spoken to any human. From my amazing perch-by-marriage at the center of the cosmological revolution, I have had the privilege of long discussions over my kitchen table or late-night drinks at conferences with some of the world's greatest scientists. At the moment of breakthrough they can feel like Moses receiving the law. Science has so much to say about the universe but no adequate name of its own for the sense of holiness and deep purpose that drives its researchers. It's an illusion of many scientists that there can be a holy grail without holiness.

But this is not nearly as dangerous as the illusion of many religious people that there can be holiness without truth.

The holy grail of science may be to explain the universe without God, but the holy grail of a flourishing scientific civilization must be to find a scientifically accurate understanding of us humans in this universe and express it, live it, and share it so that it inspires and empowers us for the future. When the arts are cut from the public schools and higher education is judged only on its income-producing potential, it's time for a new realization of what is truly sacred—or should be—to all humans. It should be a *sacred* goal to share this new vision not only mathematically but poetically, musically, mythologically, experientially, so that *anyone* can, if they choose, and at their age or intellectual level, personally come to understand and love their cosmic place in a reality that is deeper yet more convincing than all prescientific imagination. Without artists this cannot happen.

Sacred is more of a verb than an adjective. It means "we anoint." *We* determine what's sacred. By making the word *sacred* an adjective, our language has confused generations upon generations into thinking that sacredness is somehow a property of the noun that follows it, as in the phrase "sacred scripture." Our *attitude* toward something makes it sacred or not. There is nothing sacred or profane but thinking makes it so. Thus sacredness is even more important than if it were a passive characteristic of things, because, as we become aware of what is sacred to us, we discover our values and ignite our aspirations. It absolutely is possible to feel a deep relationship to the sacred while keeping our feet firmly planted in the scientific universe.

The sense of sacredness reflects our ability not only to see but to *appreciate* something to the depths of our being, to dedicate ourselves to it, and even experience awe and humility in its presence. Sacredness is linked to our god-capacity. When we talk about what's sacred to us, when we compare ideas, develop rituals to strengthen and share the act of making sacred, and above all when we live accordingly, we're cultivating this crucial ability to "anoint as sacred." If you don't think this ability is crucial, try to come up with a single person you have ever truly liked and yet for whom you can honestly say nothing was sacred.

We have the knowledge for the first time to understand that what should be sacred to all of us is *what makes us human* and gives us this extraordinary opportunity to experience self-consciousness in this universe. With education and imagination we humans can see beyond the visible objects and beings around us and comprehend how we fit into the cosmos, on all scales. What makes art, imagination, schooling, style, science, technology, and institutions that structure cooperation possible—what distinguishes us humans from our primate ancestors—is that for thousands of years we have had the drive to change things for the better and the ability to try. The power to aspire is sacred. It is the source of God. That is what we can draw on to help us carry on.

We must aspire to shape goals that are sacred for all humans, regardless of religion.

The first sacred goal is to protect our extraordinary jewel of a planet. Earth is rare, not only compared to dark matter and dark energy but compared to the *thousands* of other stardust planets that astronomers have so far discovered orbiting nearby stars. Not one of them is like our paradise planet. They're too close to their star or too far, too hot or too cold. Their orbit is highly elliptical, swinging in close to the star, then far out, creating extremely unstable conditions, or they have no liquid water or their gravity is too slight to hold an atmosphere or they hold a poisonous atmosphere or they're threatened by asteroid bombardment or by giant gas planets like Jupiter spiraling in on them or they have no moon like ours to stabilize their orbit. Something is wrong with all of them. This is not to say that some weird form of life could not have evolved on one of them, but it'd be nothing like us. It takes only a little knowledge of the history of Earth to realize that we live on a gem of the universe.

The second sacred goal is to do our best for future generations. What should "do our best" mean today? It certainly can't mean just keeping the environment from getting excessively degraded. That's a low bar for an aspiring species.

The emerging God entrusts each generation with all the knowledge that past generations have struggled to acquire, and each generation has the obligation and the opportunity to integrate its best knowledge into its collective choices, especially its laws and policies. But that isn't happening. Why? Because it is not recognized as a sacred duty.

Faith serves sacred goals when it helps us find the courage to believe the evidence, unexpected as that evidence may be, and to change to become coherent with the truth. Faith is what links us to our great-grandchildren and their world, which will still be reverberating from actions taken generations earlier—that is, actions taken now, by us. A search for shared sacredness can help us make the right decisions.

The third sacred goal is to identify with humanity's story. Everyone on Earth shares one sacred origin story—and we share much of this story with the animals. It's written in the heat radiation of the Big Bang and in ancient light arriving from distant galaxies; in fossils and geologic formations embedded in Earth; in DNA, biological evolution, and all the records of culture. The evolution of the universe, life, and ourselves is our globally shared sacred scripture, and in the last chapter is the story of God and how it emerged from the cosmically unprecedented complexity of aspiring humans. The ancients treated their stories of how their gods came into being as sacred. Those stories were told and retold ritually, from generation to generation, so that no one would ever forget. We would do well to emulate this practice.

Origin stories are not just entertainment. All cultures have used them as a template to help their members understand how they should think and live and value things.

Our cosmic origin story is not a simple one, but that's the challenge—to tell it in a way worthy of its sacredness, to lay out our expanding past and expanding future, to reveal our multiscale cosmic identities, to stun ourselves with the evidence so that we cannot help but see the sacredness of our place.

Our origin story cannot stop with our past but must reach into our own era to make viscerally clear that today is a pivotal moment for the human species, full of danger but also opportunity. After two centuries of ever-accelerating growth worldwide, humans are approaching planetary limits. The laws of physics compel a transition to a more sustainable future state. What that state will be is not yet determined, but it may depend on those of us who are here today and whether we are willing to move into scientific reality with all our furniture and make the spiritual commitment to redirect our faith to become *coherent*. We may need our god-capacity more than ever, once we grasp the enormity of the job before us. There is no deeper bond than a common origin.

You and I are the chosen people. The "chosen people" are not the members of any particular religion but *all humans alive right now*. We have been chosen by chance to be the ones whose actions will count at this pivotal moment in human evolution. What we hold sacred is what we will defend.

Humanity faces an overarching spiritual question: How can we quickly become the kind of ancestors that our descendants will be thanking for a thousand years? Here is a path. Embrace the sacred story that lets God be real and gives us a meaningful place in the universe. Embrace the immensity of the shared history that we now know unites us all and the enormous future that our planet offers. Embrace the specialness but also the urgency of our time. Rejoice as our understanding comes into sharper and sharper focus as knowledge progresses. Reject literalism, break the spiritual glass ceiling with new metaphors, find your truth box, and above all honor what is sacred to everyone.

CHAPTER 8

Planetary God, Planetary Morality

In the view of the great biologist E. O. Wilson, all debate about morality comes down to one question: Do moral guidelines come from God or did they come from the human mind? If you believe they come from God, then they are sacred and must be upheld. But if they come from the human mind *and you don't believe in evolution*, then they are just practices chosen for convenience, and we are indeed left with what is often called moral relativism, or anything goes. Evolution is the key to understanding why these are not the only alternatives.

Studies comparing several countries found that in all of them three- and four-year-olds know intuitively that hitting other people is wrong, even if they haven't been told. But the same children don't think it's wrong to shout out in class unless they have been instructed not to. So, even three-year-olds can distinguish between rules that feel moral and those that are social conventions.

In a TED talk viewed more than two million times, leading primatologist Frans de Waal shows a wonderful video of two brown capuchin monkeys in adjoining cages. They watch each other. Both have a little bowl of pebbles, and they have been trained to hand the researcher a pebble; for this they are rewarded with a slice of cucumber. Monkey 1 will do this exchange more than twenty times in a row and still enjoy the cucumber. But when monkey 2 receives a better reward (a grape, which is a more desirable food) for the same action, monkey 1 first looks bewildered, immediately hands the researcher another pebble, and becomes furious when again he gets only a cucumber. He rattles his cage, refuses to eat the cucumber, and instead hurls it at the researcher.

Like the capuchin monkeys, we too have evolved powerful emotions about fairness. We often become outraged when criminals and cheaters are not punished, even if the harm they did was not to us personally. Some apes have an even deeper moral sense than capuchins: in the same kind of experiment some have refused the grape until their partner gets one, too.

So did morality evolve?

Some philosophers claim that there's a universal morality that, under certain conditions, every rational person would agree to. But no one has ever succeeded in putting this ubermorality into words. *Without words, it's not morality*. I'm going to define *morality* very simply for the purposes of this book as "an attempt to put into words how to live with empathy and fairness to each other." The words may be in the form of rules, principles, laws, religious obligations, or taboos, or in the form of stories of characters whose actions are supposed to stand as models or inspirations for moral behavior. But the essence of morality—and of all moral guidelines or codes—is human beings struggling to *express something they already feel*.

The feeling is our evolved moral *sense*; the articulation of that is what's called a moral "code" or moral "guidelines" or a "morality." Fairness can't be defined for all circumstances. We all experience it, or its violation, in every exchange we have with each other, with groups, or with institutions, even though we would probably all define fairness differently if compelled to put it into words. This is why there have been so many moralities. If in each community we hold tightly to the idea that our version of morality came from the Creator of the Universe, then it's only logical to conclude that it must be universally true. This is the state of the world today, with dueling moralities, the believers in each averring it to be universal while in fact none of them is or could be.

Why has every culture felt compelled to convert the pure feeling of a moral sense into an explicit morality? It could be argued that morality has been used to control people, but I think the answer is that active morality—really thinking about right and wrong—is an *expression of our highest aspirations*. That's the connection between morality and a God that continually emerges from our aspirations. God didn't give us the biological urge for fairness—that urge had survival value for our primate ancestors. God is enriched by our aspirations to make cognitive sense of it.

Although other primates may have a sense of fairness, that doesn't mean that they're moral beings in the same way humans are. Expressing a morality takes cognitive ability and became possible only when our human ancestors acquired what's called fifth-order thinking—the kind of metathinking that allows us to notice how it feels to think something or allows us to put ourselves imaginatively into the mind of another person and know not only that they want fairness too but that they may not see fairness the same way we do. What allowed fifth-order thinkers to develop moralities of high complexity, de Waal believes, is our ability to symbolize and develop abstract standards, combined with an elaborate system of justification, monitoring, and punishment. These systems, he suggests, may have become the religions, so that religion is not the source of morality but a result.

Despite their aspirational source, moralities can end up being illogical and abusive, reflecting the biases and ignorance of the time. Moral codes have often been shaped to justify local power arrangements, such as the dominance of males over females, rich over poor, or one race over another, and these arrangements were anointed as God given. In medieval Europe, for example, God was believed to have personally put every living creature, from the king to the lowliest worm, in a special place of His choosing in the great chain of being. Thus if a peasant—or a female—challenged her social status, it was seen as not only quixotic but blasphemous, an insult to God. This is why moralities need to be updated as our consciousness expands.

In today's hyperconnected world, most people are exposed to so many different notions of morality—what it is, to what degree it matters, and under what circumstances—that many of us don't have any coherent belief. We find ourselves relying on intuition to cobble together a way of life that we never seriously try to explain, or, if we do try to explain it to ourselves, we keep finding reasons to make exceptions. For the first half of my life I basically lived by the seat of my pants, deciding what to do in the moment without much more than my feelings of right and wrong. Sometimes I would find myself weighing the value of doing things that seemed not quite right, repeatedly giving potential mistakes the chance to convince me to make them, and if I gave in to them, inevitably spiraling into angry disappointment in myself. Having the explicit nonreligious moral principles of the twelve steps has made my life much easier. It has definitely taught me the value of having an explicit morality, a reference point in time of trouble. Those principles protect my highest aspirations from my default tendencies, and the more automatic that choice becomes, the better. There's an old story that a grasshopper asked a centipede, "How do you coordinate all your legs?" The moment the centipede thought about it, he couldn't walk. If we had to think our way through digesting our food, we would die of starvation. Some things must be automatic. Explicit principles that work make it possible to live a more coherent daily life. Can we learn from the twelve steps how valuable it might be to have a set of nonreligious moral principles that could undergird decisions with planetary consequences?

This chapter is not about what's moral in the kind of human-to-human interactions that people have always had. It's about creating a morality on the planetary scale. We can't feel *entitled* to shape a new morality until we understand that morality is not God given.

God is emerging from the interactions of billions of aspirations, and once we start to see that, it becomes clear that God did not hand down moral laws: *we* are actually expanding God by aspiring to figure out how best to live. And we are drawing on God at the same time, through that mysterious mechanism that links an emergent phenomenon with its constituent parts. We have not only every right to start thinking about a planetary morality but a moral obligation to our descendants to try articulating what its principles could be.

WHY DO WE NEED A PLANETARY MORALITY *NOW*?

Global civilization is developing while global problems are getting worse—faster and faster. We are speeding into a new era, unfamiliar and full of danger. Without some unifying principles that are equally true for everyone on Earth, planetary-scale cooperation may be beyond reach, and those of us who are trapped in a local morality may never understand that God transcends all moralities and could unite us.

So far humanity has no successful, respectful way of combining the wills and consciences of many different kinds of people, which is the only way to serve the long-term good of Earth as a whole. Without understanding the law of the Cosmic Uroboros—that on different size scales things work differently—we will have no motivation to figure out what behavior is moral on the global scale, because *we won't know that we don't know*. We'll assume, as usual, that our good old instincts, reinforced by the people and traditions we identify with, can tell us what's right or at least acceptable. But instincts, even coupled with the best of intentions, often don't translate across size scales. In the emerging global culture our group is now the entire human species and maybe also other species. Intuition and tradition can no more tell us what is right or wrong on this scale than they can tell us what is scientifically correct.

Can there be a code of moral conduct for behavior vis-à-vis our shared planet? Can we begin to put a larger sense of fairness into words? It may actually be easier to do this for the planetary scale than for daily life, not because the issues are simpler—they're certainly not—but because there's no competition: a planetary morality doesn't obviously conflict with local moralities because most of it deals with subjects they don't recognize. What a planetary morality might do, however, is illuminate the walls of all smaller moralities' truth boxes. That might cause some conflict at the edges, but it would be invaluable.

A planetary morality would allow us to live in the consciousness of our planetary God. It would help us see that the moral *sense* that evolution gave us is sacred and limitless—but moral *action* depends on asking the right questions *for the time and place*.

Our time is a pivotal moment in the entire evolution of our species. Our place is Earth. Let's look more closely at this time and place.

In 1800 about one billion people lived on Earth, and almost everyone was poor. It had taken *tens of thousands* of years for the human population to reach that level. But the industrial revolution was beginning. Scientific revolutions and new technologies suddenly made it possible to produce vast amounts of more stuff. As people got richer, this inspired the aspirations of generation after generation, which brought about an enormous population spurt. From 1800 to today, the number of humans doubled repeatedly, quadrupling the world population during the twentieth century alone. At this writing we have shot well past seven billion. The exponential rate of population growth has slowed to not quite exponential since the 1960s, but the absolute size of the population is still zooming up. Meanwhile the rate at which *each* of us seven billion is consuming resources is also growing exponentially. The amount of carbon that people have collectively been pouring into Earth's atmosphere and oceans has *doubled every thirty years* since 1800. When you multiply exponential population growth by the exponential growth in the resources each person consumes, the last two hundred years have been a period not of growth but explosion. The explosion has been going on longer than the lifetime of anyone now living, and therefore it seems normal to us, even inevitable. But from a larger perspective it is not normal and cannot last. It's a wild aberration in the history of our species, and its continuation is by no means inevitable. In fact, it's impossible.

All that carbon is feeding the "slow-moving calamity of climate change," a phrase penned in 2012 by an anonymous poet on the *New York Times* editorial board. Climate change is a calamity moving slowly enough that, if you don't look back too far or read too much, you can comfortably burrow into the present as though the world will never change. But if you know about the past or have aspirations for your own or your children's future, you can't burrow into the shifting present any more than you can, as an adult, pull a blanket over your head and expect to become invisible.

Exponential growth builds slowly at first, then faster and faster. Unless something redirects it, it hits a limit and crashes. A few cells of green scum doubling in number each day for many months on a pond can be almost unnoticeable until one day the scum covers a quarter of the pond, the next day half the pond, and *the next day* chokes the whole pond and kills its life. By the time the effects of exponential growth become clearly visible, it may be too late to do anything about it. If business as usual continues, this is the future for us humans, and it will be painful, violent, and immoral by any standards, since we will have known and allowed it to happen anyway. Humanity's accelerating rate of growth must be checked if we want to exit this rampage with grace, justice, or any version of success. We have to believe that we are more intelligent than pond scum. How can we escape the madness of addiction to infinite growth on a finite planet? This is a moral issue with no answer in any traditional morality.

To deal with this we humans need to expand by orders of magnitude our ability to cooperate. No country or group of countries can solve a global problem, any more than putting screens on only a few of your open windows will keep out mosquitoes. Expanding cooperation may seem impossible, given the hostilities in the world today, but historically cooperation has expanded repeatedly. Figuring out how to cooperate with thousands of nonrelatives to build and maintain irrigation systems is what led to the birth of civilization five thousand years ago in Mesopotamia and Egypt. It's what saved Earth's ozone layer when 197 countries signed the Montreal Protocol in 1987, banning ozone-depleting substances. The direction of human culture has been toward larger and larger groups cooperating in one way or another—from tribes to cities to countries and soon a fully wired planet. We all live in cooperative groups and always have. Disputes happen within and between groups, and often people leave groups, but rarely do they atomize and go off to live alone. They move to or develop another group. The overriding necessity is being part of some group, and cooperating within it is the joy and also the price of membership. We all need food we can't produce ourselves. We need other humans for company. We need a culture to activate our minds, teach us language and music, and answer our burning questions. We all need protection against the slings and arrows of outrageous fortune. Cooperation is our specialty. All we need to do is extend it.

It's easy to say violence is our specialty, because it's splashy and attracts attention, but a million acts of cooperation probably take place for every act of violence. Every time a driver stops at a red light or a person gets in line, those are acts of cooperation. We don't notice the cooperation because life goes on smoothly. Few people are killers. Big killing takes a big organization and a lot of cooperation within the killing organization. Even if a group's goals are terrible, they're still good at cooperating to achieve them. Cooperation is our strength, and we should teach it, cultivate it, and exploit it. But it has to be based on a common interest and a common standard of behavior.

We need to define a new realm of morality, and nothing smaller than planetary will suffice.

A RETURN TO GOD-CAPACITY

The very possibility that Earth's entire atmosphere and oceans could overheat from people burning fossil fuels was first suggested by a daring Swedish chemist named Svante Arrhenius in the 1890s. The few people who heard that dismissed it as highly unlikely. They assumed the ocean would absorb whatever traces of carbon dioxide humans might emit. It was a huge discovery that the ocean could not do this—a discovery that required modern computers to run extremely complex models of where carbon dioxide goes and then compare the results of multiple models with difficult-to-obtain experimental results and measurements. But scientists have now done this, and we know: in the history of Earth, major climate transitions have happened several times but only over tens of thousands of years. The climate transition in process at this moment will be noticeable during a single human lifetime and change the world for children already born.

Millions of people, especially in the United States, simply refuse to believe there's a problem, despite increasingly frequent and freakish storms and heat waves, tornadoes, melting glaciers, dead coral reefs, and the silent disappearance of fish we used to eat. Even among those who don't deny climate change, great numbers of influential people still don't grasp the accelerating rate at which this and other human-caused changes are happening.

As economic growth and climate change push Earth's limits, we can foresee the possibility of desperate wars, migrations, and plagues. Without any common understanding of our plight on this planet, there will be no basis for agreement on how to mitigate disasters. Everyone will look out for themselves. As the pace of events accelerates, mistakes will be magnified according to principles of chaos theory. If the exponential growth ends with a crash, what will it look like? Chaotic and deadly? Isn't the moral course to try to make the transition as gentle and just as we can?

Many today assume that the momentum of climate change is unstoppable because changing *other* people's habits is impossible. They have leaped straight from denial to despair. Or perhaps to planning how they can profit from the coming change—or at least barricade their family against its effects. The poor will feel the effects of climate change first, but the rich will feel it shortly thereafter. We may minimize our moral discomfort by saying "people will adapt," but there's a limit to how technologically adapted our descendants can become if there's a runaway greenhouse effect. It may have been a runaway greenhouse effect that left Venus with temperatures above 800 degrees, an atmosphere full of carbon dioxide, clouds of poison gas, and rock hot enough to melt lead.

I'm not trying to make anyone live in fear. Fear is painful while accomplishing nothing. It's a complete failure as a motivating force. It doesn't lead to creativity but to hunkering down in the known. But there's a difference between fear and reality. I'm pointing out reality. Reality is the subject of this book. *How God can be part of it.* If we want God, we have to look for it in reality. What should be done about climate change is up for debate, but that it's happening is simply reality.

We need to have better concepts to approach the reality of the long term. If you were to throw a bowling ball off a skyscraper, could you say that the consequences to the person it crushed on the ground were not your fault because you weren't thinking of things that far away? Of course not. But this is what many of us do with respect to time rather than space. In a world focused on the quarterly report or the next election, people don't think very far ahead in time. When I worked on the staff of Congress, we used to calculate the costs of various policy alternatives to people not yet born. But if the consequences to those future people are deemed essentially an economic calculation, then, following the economic rationale I mentioned earlier, the present value of those future humans (like the present value of an inheritance that may not be received for decades) is discounted. Their lives are worth less financially than ours and are discounted more the further into the future they will live. Once they're far enough off to get discounted to almost zero, they are no longer a concern or even seen. This kind of thinking drastically stunts our conception of the future.

The truth is, the kind of destruction that today's practices are setting on course may harm not only the worlds of our own children and grandchildren, not only the next ten thousand years but the entire future of the galaxy. If we degrade our descendants' world enough so that they never explore space, we could abort the future of intelligence in the visible universe. What is *that* worth?

No culture, no religion, and no political ideology has an answer. None of them has yet seriously considered, let alone developed, a moral understanding that *accurately* spans size scales and timescales. But this is what we need for the emerging global civilization. There are higher values than loyalty to any particular religion. God is not finished evolving yet, not by a long shot, and neither is our moral understanding. The evolved moral sense that all humans share is sacred, but we have to expand what we do with it by using the best knowledge and widest and most accurate perspective we have.

Our problem is actually even bigger than saving the planetary conditions in which we humans thrive. It's about saving our souls. There will be fights about the money to pay for increasingly frequent disasters from hurricanes, floods, fires, and tornadoes; we could fall into a financial black hole. But what scares me far more is that if climate catastrophes become the norm, we may gradually become numb to each other's suffering. There's a limit to how many times anyone can respond with empathy and cash. We may burn out. Emotional vulnerability may become a luxury we can't afford psychologically. If, in the long term, it becomes more conducive to survival and reproduction to steel oneself against the flood of pain outside, then evolution will take our descendants in that direction.

The survival of compassion is at risk with climate change. Can you imagine a world without compassion?

If this is not a moral issue, I don't know what is.

We are up against a problem that may never have existed in the history of the universe. It may be that no other intelligent aliens exist or, if they do, that they have never evolved to collectively take over a planet the way we have. In which case, there is absolutely no telling what will happen as we approach the end of exponential growth here on Earth. There is no role model.

> *How can our group behave respectfully but cautiously toward other groups that have their own aspirations, however bad those aspirations may seem to us?*
>
> *How can we individually expand our moral sense to care about our collective effects at size scales and timescales we are just beginning to grasp?*

God won't hand us a plan. No list of technologies and work orders for the world will descend full blown into our praying brains. But God draws big aspirations out of us and feeds us the spiritual oxygen to live them out. Every tiny detail of the rescue of our planet has been or will be contributed by some invaluable individual, but if we can extend cooperation enough, the whole of how it happens will be an emergent phenomenon. Like God.

A moral shift can happen with a return to our god-capacity. When we are hopeless and powerless in an addiction—as the world is today, deep in its addiction to economic growth at any cost—the solution requires a greater vision. A new big picture. The industrial revolution gave people a new and powerful set of aspirations that changed the world and lifted many people out of poverty, but now we have to expand our aspirations in a very different direction, based on everything we have learned and seen since then. Now the challenge is to shape a materially sustainable world where most growth is in knowledge, justice, compassion, creativity, and spiritual connection.

SHARABLE PRINCIPLES OF A PLANETARY MORALITY

The purpose of a planetary morality would not be to tell anyone what to do but simply to agree on long-term ideals and establish motivation. With no more than ideals and motivation, there are plenty of smart people who will be able to figure out what to do, but without ideals and motivation, no number of smart people can succeed.

What form would a planetary morality take? It would have to be a set of broad principles, not prescriptive rules. Life is far too complex and fluid for there ever to be enough rules. Principles, on the other hand, express aspirations. They're the opposite of rules, and that's their merit. But principles are a challenge to apply. There's no single way in any given case. The facts matter. The situation calls for perception and judgment. Negotiation is desirable. But this is what we have big brains for. Planetary moral principles should not tell us what to do but suggest *how to envision and what to cultivate*.

I will suggest a few principles of a planetary morality. (I won't attempt to list smaller-scale ones, since we will probably find them inside the truth boxes of our religions.) Without changing anything else, if the world could agree on these general principles, we could be freed of the conflicting universal gods and their moralities, and we could almost certainly find enough common ground to cooperate in solving our global problems. The point of a planetary morality is to make *explicit* the things we want always to remember and hold sacred. Above all, to remember.

1. Earth is extraordinarily special in the evolving double dark universe, and beings like us may be rare or even unique in the cosmos and must be protected.
2. Truth is the only foundation for a sharable, coherent picture of reality.
3. It took almost the entire age of the universe, 13.8 billion years, for us to evolve, and our descendants could live comfortably on Earth for another billion years; the twenty-first century is

the pivotal moment when human decisions will make that future possible or impossible.

4. For a sustainable future our current exponential rate of resource use must end and become slow material growth supported by boundless creativity; we must do more with less.
5. Emergent phenomena are inevitable as any situation becomes
   substantially larger or more complex, so anticipate them, accept them, work with them, and be humble before reality.
6. There is one magnificent cosmic origin story, and it is equally
   true for everyone on Earth. To know who we are, we must tell
   it in every language, every medium, and every generation.
7. We humans may be the beginning of a multibillion-year blossoming of intelligence in the visible universe, so let's act as if
   we are. Let's think of ourselves as the hottest start-up ever.
8. God emerges from our aspirations, so embrace aspirations
   worthy of the kind of God you want.

In a planetary morality we would think of future people as real—
part of our species and thus part of us. Because that's what they are.
They're just not here yet. But they need a few representatives now.
Every person who appreciates this *is* one of their representatives and
is playing a cosmic role. You can be an advocate for our species and,
by extension, our cosmos. We're not here just for our individual
selves. We're here today, whether we realize it or not, representing an evolutionary presence that has been flowering for a hundred
thousand years and could continue through our descendant species
for hundreds of millions more.

We are in the cosmic congress—that is, alive—representing our
constituents, past, present, and future, all of whom have an active
interest in protecting Earth. (Yes, even the dead have an active interest. Their aspirations are still part of the emerging God, which
would cease to exist if humanity died out.) Taking or even allowing
actions that threaten the human species drains all the meaning out
of our large-scale lives right now, since it assumes the future doesn't

count, that it's not part of who we are, that we're here, sitting in congress, with no constituents. That we are a charade.

We are here to lead. Not that we're particularly well qualified—we've been chosen by chance. Nevertheless it's a huge honor—*or so we can see it.* We are the ones who have appeared at this moment, and the responsibility is ours to open our consciousness to the state of the world, contribute whatever we can, and realize that in the coming decades of trial by fire on this planet only a God that is real can really help us.

WHAT ABOUT ME?

You may be wondering, "What does all this have to do with me? I'm willing to help, but the state of the world is not my problem. I didn't melt the Arctic!"

Of course you didn't. But assuming a defensive stance is not without cost.

You are responsible for the direction of your species in exactly the same way that you are connected to God: in both cases you are part of an emergent phenomenon. I've come to see that if I want my connection with God to feel real, my connection to my species has to feel real, too. The more willingly I accept my complicity, however small, in our species' troubles, the more viscerally I begin to experience what it means to be actively and consciously participating in a larger emergent reality. Actively and consciously participating in a larger emergent reality is how we connect to God. God too is a collective phenomenon, and we can *discover* how to feel connected and how to cultivate that connection.

Suppose a planetary morality encouraged us to accept our tiny but real role in humanity's collective troubles; our role in its enormous potential and future would also start feeling real and accessible. There is no limit to how empowering that consciousness could be. The emerging God *compels* us to open our minds to the collective scale, because it's on the collective scale that God is real. When each of us comes to understand our part in climate change, painful though it is to acknowledge, this has the surprising side benefit of revealing what it means to be playing a role in emergence—and helps us to feel ourselves a living part of an emerging God.

The very existence of this God is challenging us to experience the new universe in its strange yet believable vitality and to feel the sacred connections between it and every one of us. When we aspire to share the meaning of those connections with each other as clearly and generously as we can, God is emerging right here between us.

God becomes present and potentially empowering the moment we grasp that we intelligent beings are playing roles in *many* emergent phenomena much bigger than ourselves. We are playing a role in our culture with every word we speak; we are playing a role in our nation's wars even when we oppose them; we are playing a role in the evolution of our species if we raise or don't raise children; we are playing a role in our own afterlives with decisions we're making today. The melding of those kinds of roles is our large-scale identity. If we remain unaware of them or reject them as too much trouble, we cut ourselves down to a fraction of our true selves and will live forever confused and in conflict with others' equally small identities, each of us claiming to uphold some traditional morality that can't answer our most pressing questions. If, however, we understand that our full selves encompass many collective roles, we begin to grasp emotionally why we need a planetary moral perspective and the sooner the better.

The more clearly we humans come to understand the universe and its immense history, the more we can come into harmony with it in our thinking about what is moral and in our felt sense of what's real, including God. The more we are in harmony with the universe and God, the more sustainable—even regenerating—our lives will be. We'll experience taking the long view not as sacrifice but as oneness and fulfillment and harmony with God—because that's what it is.

Around the world even traditional ideas of morality are still changing, if painfully slowly. At least the expectation is no longer widespread, as it was in the ancient world, that those who win a war have the right to take the losers and their children home as slaves. We humans are still trying to figure out how to live with each other. Ideals like democracy; rationalism; rights for women, gay people, the disabled, and oppressed people of all kinds have in the past century or two spread surprisingly fast. But that's not enough. Accelerating global challenges are quickly making the need for cooperation a life-or-extinction issue. This means we must start focusing now on developing a rudimentary planetary morality. It needs to be based on what is exactly the same for every human being on Earth: our evolved characteristics plus our reliable knowledge.

We humans are the peak of complexity in the known universe, but we're by no means finished. Each of us is a complex process, like a galaxy: its stars live and die, everything is in motion, but the galaxy persists. It's the same with our bodies. Our cells live and die, all our atoms are in motion, but we persist. It's the same with our species. Individuals live and die, we're all in motion, but the species persists. Once we see ourselves as a four-dimensional reality across time, we realize that we *are* our future and our past right now. We all are.

We're part of something thrilling and unfathomable that may never have happened before in the entire galaxy, or the universe for all we know, and may never happen again. There could be an enormous future for our descendants. New stars and planetary systems will keep forming in the galaxy for billions of years. If our descendants gradually *move* Earth farther from the sun as the sun inevitably heats up (astronomers have already figured out theoretically how to do this), and if our descendants eventually expand off this planet, they and their descendant species could go on for a *trillion* years. That is, if they remain creative enough to keep tuning their biological moral sense to the world they're actually living in. We can set them on that path. We have a God at last that could help unite us in the rescue of our planet, our civilization, and our future. Dedicating ourselves to that, openly, willingly, exuberantly, would be a moral act worthy of our time.

CHAPTER 9

A Big Picture for Our Time

The last time anyone in the West had a coherent big picture that pulled together God, the universe, and daily life was the Middle Ages, and it was possible then only because so little was known and so much imagined. The Middle Ages effectively ended when Galileo was silenced by the Catholic Church under threat of torture for teaching what was in fact the truth. Science and religion parted ways. God lost His physical place in the scientific universe but remained an ineradicable part of our psyches, so that the battleground between science and religion was now inside us. Largely because of science and technology, the pace of change in our lives has continued to accelerate and is now so fast that the pressures on each of us can feel overwhelming, but our images of God have barely changed at all. Our thinking about God today is like a potted plant that's root-bound and can barely grow. The pot is made of old metaphors, images, and stories. Not only are science and spirituality not necessarily antagonistic but science may be the only way to break out of the pot and put our spiritual roots into Earth and the cosmos, where they can grow freely. Where they can be coherent with reality.

The almost unquestioned assumption since the time of Galileo has been that religion defines good and evil, while science is neutral on values and simply provides the power to do whatever we choose. But when it comes to the long-term future of humanity, it turns out the opposite is true. Science is making possible our broadest understanding of good and evil: the good is actions and systems that further the survival and continuing evolution of intelligent life; the bad is what threatens it. But defining the good doesn't necessarily make it happen; we all know that science has also enabled terrible things on enormous scales. We need our god-capacity to generate the spiritual power—the motivation, trust, and faith in each other—to bring good about. How we conceive of God will have enormous impact on how we behave toward each other, how we justify our actions, what we believe is possible, and what we find sacred and are therefore willing to sacrifice to protect.

The fundamental mistake that sabotages the possibility of a coherent big picture is insisting that God be all powerful. Because nothing real can be *all* anything. To be real it must be limited. The visible universe has limits. Time has limits. The Big Bang has limits. If there's something infinite beyond the Big Bang, as some cosmologists speculate, it has nothing to do with us. It's not *our* God.

Let's take back our power and invest it better. If we are going to have a God capable of helping us survive, we're going to have to take more responsibility for discerning what it is or might be. Relying on the Creator of the Universe to save humanity is like slapping a car with a buggy whip and expecting it to go faster.

If our ideas about God are not helping us to experience, cherish, and protect our special place on this planet in this universe but are instead permitting us—or, worse, helping us—to degrade our children's world, then we need a new understanding of God. We need a God that can connect us spiritually to the real universe and guide our now globally conscious species toward a long-term and honorable civilization.

Today the ways that god-capacity is being exercised are too frequently counterproductive, and aggressively so, by people whose ignorance or denial of the state of the world is leading our species and thousands of other species toward disaster. As Yeats warned, "The best lack all conviction, while the worst / Are full of passionate intensity." We all have limitless spiritual power, but many of us, constrained by the high standards of modern scientific civilization, have been unable to access that spiritual power so long as it seemed inconsistent with reality. Honoring those constraints has paid off. For the first time we can have a *coherent* picture of reality that meets our highest scientific standards, reveals unexplored terrain in ourselves, has a meaningful place for an awesome God, and frees our spirits to strike out with fervor—and not a moment too soon.

Every one of us has the ability to draw power from the emerging God and commit ourselves with astonishing energy to live up to our highest aspirations, but we can't do it without a believable big picture that tells us who we are and *why we should*. We need a big picture that makes sense of the high-tech, fast-paced, and dangerous world we're actually living in, in the context of our evolutionary history, our planet, and the universe. Without a coherent believable big picture, there is no way to conceptualize the whole and thus *no way to see reality*. No way to ever find a real God.

Without a story that makes sense of our many-leveled world by showing us how we fit into it, millions of us can't tap into our smoldering potential because we remain confused about what to commit ourselves to or how. The old stories do not touch our world. Our god-capacity has been left in suspended animation.

We need a coherent big picture that is equally true for every human being and gives us a convincing and inspiring God that is consistent with everything we know and every truth we will learn. Incoherence between beliefs and goals on the one hand and modern knowledge on the other is what many religious people are endlessly struggling to overcome with faith. Coherence eliminates the struggle. We can claim our cosmic pasts, aspire to the future, and still be fully here now. We can speak to God and hold a scientific worldview. It's all coherent.

But coherence doesn't arrive as a matter of grace, like a sudden spiritual experience. It takes a sustained decision to want it. Coherence is the sweet spot of a full existence. When you hit that sweet spot, you are touching God—you're experiencing your actions, beliefs, knowledge, and feelings as one reality, which of course they are. When we're experiencing what *of course* is, we're in harmony with the universe.

It's time to wake up our god-capacity. Human beings will never share a big picture that leaves out God—but we can never share a God that many of us know isn't real. We have a stunning new scientific story of the cosmos, the first ever based on evidence, but science alone does not provide a coherent big picture. A God that is real is the missing link to a big picture for our time.

Science is not a spiritual path, but it can be a spiritual technology—a kind of spaceship. It's not the journey or the destination or the purpose, but without a solidly built spaceship all those are pipe dreams. I'm trusting my life to this spaceship, because wouldn't you rather trust your life to a vehicle designed by scientists and engineers than to one designed by scriptural experts? In practice everyone trusts their life to science, even if in their conscious minds they hold an utterly inconsistent view. The most fanatic literalists nevertheless fly on airplanes, even if once they land, they preach that scientific thinking is a hoax. Terrorists whose narrow religious worldview logically precludes the principles on which modern science and technology are based nevertheless spew hate through the Internet and rely on cell phones to trigger explosions. These people are incoherent to the core, and their lives sow discord. People can and should disagree about what's good or bad, or what we should do collectively, but it's dangerous for society to disagree about the nature of reality itself *when the facts are already known*. This is a setup for mass incoherence.

It's time to ask, What do we humans really need from our idea of God? What kind of God, if any, will be most conducive to making us useful to the world, giving us peace of mind, and showing us how to live in harmony with the universe and with each other? We need to find such a God, because all future generations are depending on us.

The message is simple: If we cling to a vision of God that forces us to think in primitive ways, we are doomed to smallness, bickering, and perhaps extinction. But if we let God be real, with all that that entails, then we can live in the real universe, with God's real help, as full cosmic beings, and this identity will not only cohere with our daily lives but will also illuminate them.

Collectively we are influencing God. The worse we behave, measured against our own deepest aspirations, the weaker God becomes, not only for us but for future generations. The better we act, the richer God becomes and the more useful to future generations. We have the power to strengthen the very God we turn to. This is a pretty amazing investment opportunity. Collectively we can strengthen God, and then, when we need it, which will happen, it will be much better at strengthening us.

The spiritual challenge for us is to accept the scientific picture of the universe and with the real help of a real God figure out *how to act accordingly*—in every way, not just technologically but sociologically, psychologically, spiritually, educationally, politically, and every other way. It may not be obvious how to become this coherent, but for the first time it's possible, and focusing on it as a goal could reenergize our civilization.

We have the opportunity to use our god-capacity for a high purpose—truly a cosmic purpose: to find ourselves and save the million-year-old, still evolving cosmic clan in which each of us is a living organism.

Yeah, sure.

Cynicism about a "new view of God" is practically automatic in our society, with many people simply shrugging, convinced that society's short-term thinking is unfortunately inevitable, and therefore we're probably doomed to destroy ourselves. We've all heard the scientific-sounding excuse that evolutionary strategies are only concerned with short-term survival (long enough to reproduce), and thus humans don't, and never will, understand the long term. But our minds are not so limited. We're always reaching new levels of thinking in justice, communication, technology, conservation, and so on. And we're building on what earlier people achieved—inventing clothing, taming fire, forming societies, developing art, writing, science, metaphor, institutions. Not one of those things was created for the exclusive purpose of breeding. We're *always* aspiring.

Cynicism involves disdain for those who have faith in other people, but it's an incoherent stance, because cynics are in practice entirely supported by their faith in other people—faith, that is, that the rest of society will continue to produce food, keep the electricity and entertainment flowing, protect them from violence, and pay them their salaries. All of us, actually, live only through faith in other people. Our pop cultural trend toward cynicism (and its cousins, snark and irony) will pass. Cynicism currently is considered smart and cool, certainly cooler than sincerity and often cooler than idealism. But on the scale of evolution, cynicism is not a survival strategy, and it cannot last.

Because it's wrong on the facts. For millions of years our ancestors *always* rose to the challenge—every challenge—or we would not be here today. Humans carry the genes of the fittest, not the losers. We have, genetically wired into our every cell, a multibillion-year readiness to adapt in order to survive. *Inevitably* people will adapt. What seems unbearable and impossible today could become something we're absolutely willing to adapt to if it will save us. But that willingness could come too late. The challenge is to use foresight to adapt *now*, while we still have highly desirable choices and the power to carry them out.

You don't have to be a cynic, though, to be skeptical. Perhaps you feel the call to a coherent worldview, but a new God seems like a dangerous step. What if the idea is wrong? Could God punish you? You're not alone in this concern.

When the seventeenth-century French philosopher Blaise Pascal found out that the heavenly spheres did not exist and that there was no place in the new cosmos for God, he acknowledged that maybe God didn't exist; however, he reasoned, since we can't know for sure, we have to choose whether to believe. This was his logic:

if you believe and God doesn't exist, you've lost nothing, but if He exists and you don't believe, you may pay for your mistake throughout all eternity, so the safer bet is to believe. "Pascal's wager" still reverberates in the thinking of countless people today who worry that if they question God's existence or power or nature, even in the privacy of their minds, He will notice their disloyalty, and they will suffer some form of divine retribution, either in this life or the next, endangering their salvation. They tell themselves, as Pascal did, that it's safer to stick with belief in the traditional God, just in case He exists, since if He doesn't, no harm done. That's where they make their mistake. Because immense harm is done: They're throwing away all opportunity for real salvation in the real universe. There is no possibility of retribution from God. Retribution will be delivered by Earth. It's already begun. But the emerging God can help us to be and do the best we can in the face of that.

People who plan to save their own souls without doing anything to protect the whole—or, worse, who contribute to its demise—should rethink their strategy. They're acting like a brain that assumes it doesn't need the rest of the body, so it decides to ignore the body's demands. How long would that brain live? How long would it even stay sane? In the same way that a brain and a body stay alive only if they stay together, salvation is a collective goal. It will come for humanity and our God, or it will evade us all.

A NEW IDENTITY

Each of us is a process that takes a lifetime, but when we look at the world and each other, we see only two-second clips. From a cosmic perspective, every one of us is actively playing a part in many emergent phenomena, like a language, a culture, an economy, perhaps an industry, a political or social movement, an electorate. The most difficult emergent phenomenon to face our role in may be climate change. The most amazing is God. We're not just a person with an interesting backstory; in some sense each of us *is* this unique story unfolding, grabbing hold of whatever atoms and energy are nearby to act it out.

No one has any identity, except across time. We all value things based on not only what they physically are in this instant but on what we know about their history. If we thought of things as being only what's scientifically measurable at this moment, we would lose all ability to value them, since equivalent substitutes could always be manufactured. A natural and a manufactured diamond, for example, can be visually and even chemically identical, but if you know which is which, you'll always prefer the natural one. The same is true of antiques. In Israel I once bought a replica of a simple clay oil lamp from the time of Abraham that looked identical to genuinely ancient ones that were on sale for many times the price. But I regret it. It would have been worth it to have paid many times as much for the object with history, because history stimulates the imagination, and everyone needs that. The history of objects—that is, something inherent not in them but in our way of thinking about them—can make them more precious. Or it can destroy their value, like the land that lay fallow for half a century in the middle of Berlin where the Gestapo headquarters, long gone, had stood. Once we realize that the history of everything makes it what it is, we need to start looking not just at objects but at ourselves and each other that way.

Like every star, every galaxy, the cosmos itself, each of us is an event unfolding predictably on some scales and unpredictably on others. We are our history all the way back, through the evolution of mammals to strange creatures in the sea to the first cells, through the deaths of stars that made our stardust, through the swirling dark matter that made the galaxy in which our sun could ignite. We humans have traveled a long road together since the Big Bang.

It's time to acknowledge that.

New information alone rarely changes anyone's thinking, let alone their behavior. Information can come in the form of a million sticky notes stuck on your skull, altering nothing underneath. The way to change deeply and lastingly is to take on a new identity that gives us an exciting role in a larger, more inspiring story and associates us with people who inspire and welcome us. On finding a new identity people can become willing almost overnight to make huge changes in their lives to be the bigger person they suddenly realize they can be. This is how people fall in love, how religious conversions occur, and how addicts recover.

What could truly transform us now into the kind of people we need to become is our newly discovered cosmic identity. It's available, it's infinitely expansive, and it connects us to all people—regardless of religion, race, or nationality. In our cosmic identity we are part of God and loyal to the human species—not simply to the individuals here today but to the aspirations of our ancestors and potential of our descendants into the distant future. Our minds expand to encompass the very long term, and we experience ourselves as part of it. We have humanity's first real chance to achieve what the ancients sought above all else—harmony with the universe. Only now it's harmony with the planet and the double dark universe.

Earth doesn't see us humans as individuals, any more than we see water as molecules. Earth sees us as a powerful force and a part of itself, and we need to accept that, from a certain point of view, we are indeed that. What does it mean to be part of Earth? Some of us may not actually feel much like part of Earth, especially if we live in a big noisy city and are scarcely conscious of nature. Am I less a part of Earth than the wild animals? After all, they experience no doubts on the subject. Am I less a part than a person who *feels* more a part? Does my mental state determine to what extent I am embedded in Earth? I know when I was a city dweller I would have said yes, feeling quite a bit less embedded (or so I assumed) than those who live close to the land. But by changing our attitudes we can begin to feel our embeddedness in Earth. We can *become* Earth *in our own minds*. This certainly displays a mental dimension of Earth's. If what Earth's parts *are* is determined by how they *feel*, then Earth is feeling. Through us. We are the self-consciousness of Earth.

We are also the self-consciousness of the universe, as far as any-one knows. There might be self-conscious aliens somewhere out there with their own emergent gods and developing their own brand of intelligence—but what if there aren't? Without us and our God the universe could be just sound and fury, signifying nothing. In biblical times God was believed to live in a tent on a mountain-top or in the clouds; in the Middle Ages God was believed to live outside the sphere of the fixed stars; but in the double dark evolving universe, God lives in the diamond mine of self-consciousness we call planet Earth.

Every one of us shares the incredibly rich identity forged over the billions of years it took for us to evolve out of this planet in this universe. We're unique loving individuals; we're an Earth-encircling force; we're the living ancestors of descendants who may change the galaxy; we're part of the self-consciousness of the universe; our aspirations are part of God and will be as long into the future as God exists. This is the real us. Identity is about *daring* to define ourselves. Why would we choose a limiting self-definition? How many chances do we think we'll get? That we are cosmic be-ings is the core of our identity. We will share this *forever*. The rest is local color.

What if we could actually remember this? What if we could re-member that the universe exists on all size scales, all the time, and that most of it is spiritual? What if we felt as surely as we feel gravity that there's a meaningful place for us in the cosmic order and that God is here and present if we just think about it a different way?

OPENING THE DOOR TO GOD

In a famous series of TV interviews, the journalist Bill Moyers rhe-torically asked the mythologist Joseph Campbell, "Doesn't everyone want to know the meaning of life?" and Campbell surprised him by answering, "No, they want the experience of it!" We all want the ex-perience of living intensely, to feel truly alive and part of something big and meaningful and challenging. Some veterans actually miss war when they come home, because nothing measures up to the intensity, purpose, and sense of aliveness in the face of death. This was captured perfectly in a *Doonesbury* comic by Garry Trudeau. One vet confesses to the other that he misses Afghanistan. Not that Afghanistan is his home: war is his home.

> "And your real home?"
> "Sir, my real home is AT&T bills and couples counseling."
> "Mine, too, but isn't that what we're fighting for?"

While today's cool and ironic attitude mocks those who advocate higher goals, these young vets are literally dying for higher goals— but they don't know what the real choices are. There is something much higher than patriotism. No religion can explain the enormous climate transition now happening on Earth or the enormous material transition about to happen as the exponential resource growth of the past two centuries approaches its limit. No religion can inspire young people even to understand, let alone to lead, these transitions. No known religion yet emphasizes what really matters: identifying with the human species, seeing its challenges as our own, seeking knowledge of our planetary moral involvement, and demanding that God be a real player in this cosmic drama.

For the price of accepting, with no holding back, our honest share of responsibility in our species' troubles, the door to the higher level opens and God is available. Every time we allow ourselves to accept the terror and regret of Earth's problems, opening our minds and spirits to the *collective* pain and the *collective* fate, we are opening our consciousness to the place where God is real and present and awe inspiring. Why would anyone not take that deal? Every time we let ourselves *feel* the reality of this cosmos and experience the certainty that "I'm not just 'me.' *I'm the human species passing through me,*" we are priming ourselves for divine contact.

Umm, wait. Does this mean that making a spiritual connection to the emerging God will cost us a big chunk of our personal happiness, because we'll be weighed down by the problems of the world?

No, fortunately that's not how it works.

I have known several people who told me they didn't want to bring children into this world because it was too messed up. I knew one woman who was contemplating suicide after years of fighting for environmental causes because she felt it was hopeless. These people are truly suffering, but from what? I think it's from *emotional scale confusion.* Our emotions didn't evolve for the kind of world we live in today. Our ancestors lived in small tribes and felt emotions about people and animals they knew. But today we're inundated with news of everything wrong around the planet, much of it statistical and thus abstract but still evoking powerful emotions when we understand their implications. So now, as we are learning to *think* about more than one size scale, we also need to learn to *feel*—consciously—on more than one size scale. Our feelings don't have to be consistent across all size scales. Nothing else in the universe is. Coherent doesn't mean consistent; it means *scale appropriate.* The kind of emotion we would feel at the news that our child has been in a car accident is not appropriate when we hear the news that the amount of carbon in the atmosphere has exceeded four hundred parts per million, even though the carbon will affect far more children. What's a useful feeling about events on one scale is rarely useful about events on another.

Our job is to live with joy while doing everything we can to improve the odds for our descendants and our planet. Joy increases motivation. Our best hope is energized, not demoralized, people who are vigorously and creatively attacking large-scale problems while guiltlessly living fun, loving lives on the small scale. And doing so whether we seem to be succeeding on the large or not. As the political activist Emma Goldman is reputed to have said: "If I can't dance, I don't want to be part of your revolution."

DAY LANGUAGE/NIGHT LANGUAGE

A new understanding of God doesn't mean we toss out all the profound concepts and beautiful expressions of earlier visions of God. They are, like art, part of the legacy of culture and thus part of the emerging God. But we need to reinterpret them. Spiritual imagery that helps us feel cosmically connected is invaluable and always will be but only if it makes us feel connected to the *real* cosmos. A big picture has to be expressed artistically and emotionally. We need mythological language—what the visionary writer Michael Dowd calls "night language," as opposed to the "day language" of facts and rational discourse. Day language and night language are two sides of the same coin, and the coin is us. The "two cultures" view of society—that is, the view that science and the humanities are forever at odds—misguidedly encourages the two sides of our being to fight for dominance and resources. But neither could have created our world without the other, and neither can sustain it alone. Rational versus irrational, natural versus supernatural, science versus religion—all are gross oversimplifications that result at least in part from taking night language too literally. The emerging God can have all the power and beauty of earlier ideas of God if we understand our *need* for night language. We can talk *about* God in day language but talk *to* God in night language.

Here are three random examples of spiritual concepts, expressed in night language, that are central to the twelve-step programs. When I look at them in light of the emerging God, they make a new kind of sense. I will use the first person here, because the intimacy of these ideas is important and because no doubt there are other ways to interpret them and still arrive at the same destination: reality.

God's will, not mine, be done.

This prayer is hugely useful to millions of people. But what does "God's will" mean? The emerging God's will is the interaction of *our* plans—at least our aspirations: our hopes, the best we can imagine. The moment I turn to God rather than to just what's in front of my eyes, I expand my perspective to try to see anew from the collective consciousness. I commit to thinking cosmically. This change of perspective almost always improves the behavior choices apparent to me. The "not mine" in that phrase refers to my unexamined default behavior, which is probably either some bad habit or confusion—and such behaviors are what this prayer is aiming to transcend.

Turn your will and life over to a higher power.

The idea of "turning over" your life or "surrendering" (another way of putting it) to a higher power utterly mystified me when I first heard it. Not only did I not know how to turn anything over—I couldn't imagine why I should want to. I was too literal.

"Turning over to" a higher power or God doesn't mean I'm a weakling looking for fantasy help, as I originally assumed. When I know that God is emerging from my own deepest aspirations, turning my will over to that God means returning to my true aspirations, which I have postponed or allowed to become clouded. It means to become willing to live according to the way I most deeply aspire to be, whether I believe that's possible or not. Living as *I aspire* to live. This is the biggest victory. It's giving up the excuses, the rationales, the procrastination, and facing that I have one life and the only time to live it as I aspire to is now. When I pray to "know God's will for me," I am really praying to know my full self on all its emergent levels, to take in my larger identity as the human race right here where I sit, to respect and love the whole thing, to see my personal path, and commit to stay centered on it. I am essentially saying, Let me be guided by the best aspirations my species has to offer, and help me see what that means.

Am I trying to live the way God wants me to live?

Am I giving up on myself because my own aspirations seem too demanding? "The way God wants me to live" is based not on the social atmosphere of the moment with its fads and pressures; it's based on who we deeply are, the abilities that our ancestors and our education have bequeathed us, and the needs of our time. Sometimes people do harmful things because they have bad aspirations, but most of the bad things people do they do *despite* their deepest aspirations, not because of them. We are complex, and our aspirations don't always drive us. Sometimes we haven't even figured out what they are, and sometimes, even if we have, people and conditions around us seem to force us down other paths. This question helps clarify aspirations and put them in control, if we understand that this is how it works.

Most of the world's religious imagery is night language, the purpose of which is to evoke feeling, not communicate literal content. Day and night language, scientific reality and God—there are no seams between them. The emerging God, after all, is the source of *all* meaning, old and new, and can be understood this way in *any* religion that doesn't require taking its teachings literally.

THE PROMISED LAND

We who are alive today are the Moses generation. We're laying the groundwork for the Promised Land. None of us will get to enter the Promised Land—it's far off in the future—but we're the ones making the promises. All of us are responsible to the future of our species as a whole, because it took the evolution of the whole species to create us. The challenge is to recognize that we have this enormous identity and to take charge of our situation—to know that we are the species acting to preserve itself—although only by the grace of individual heroes will it actually happen.

But what exactly are we promising future generations? Conflict for the many on a degrading planet, while a few exploit technology for small ends?

We can make better promises:

> Awakening to the emerging God promises us love on previously unknown scales—for Earth and the cosmos, for the immensity of what it took to create us, and for all the children to come.
>
> It promises us a huge identity that spans all time. It *reveals* that identity. We are going to know what we truly are, not just what we need to be in order to function in the lifestyle of today's society.
>
> The emerging God can resurrect for the modern age the sense of unmediated power that shamans once drew directly from their felt connection to nature, but for us "nature" includes everything from the Planck length to the cosmic horizon.
>
> We will see all humans, including ourselves, as flowers on the same great tree, sharing almost all our DNA and absolutely all our cosmic history even with those most different from us.
>
> We will intuitively understand how the future of our descendants depends on the future of their descendants.
>
> We will experience how being human fits smoothly and perfectly into the evolution of a meaningful yet scientifically supported universe.
>
> We will see both global and personal problems from a new perspective that diminishes them and reveals unexpected means to solve them.
>
> We will realize that heaven and hell are not the fates of individuals but rather potential futures for our species.
>
> We will welcome every discovery of science as bringing us more fully into reality, because once we let God be real, no scientific truth can ever be in conflict with God, so no truth need ever be feared or denied.
>
> We will suddenly realize that the emerging God is doing for us what we could never do for ourselves.

How can all this happen from a mere idea? There are certain ideas that, once grasped, change everything. I experienced it almost thirty years ago when I discovered that I was not fatally flawed; I simply had an illness called compulsive eating, and there was a solution called recovery. This same realization has launched enormous transformations of personality and worldview for millions of people addicted to all kinds of things, from shopping and gambling to drugs and alcohol. Yet a realization is just a new idea. It's free. The realization that God has emerged from humanity in a meaningful way and is infinitely complex yet in direct contact with each of us could launch a transformation as total as recovery from addiction.

There is something real that is worthy of the name God. Those of us who could never understand God before, because we had been exposed only to dubious images of God, can at last open our minds. We can free ourselves from the rejection of all things spiritual, which once seemed mandatory for a rational outlook but has in fact diminished our belief in ourselves and suppressed what should have been our evolutionary war cry for survival.

The emerging God is, I suppose, radical by the standards of the moment, but in fact I am a profoundly conservative person. I'm trying to conserve this vital experiment, perhaps unique in all the cosmos—the evolution of intelligent life and complex societies on this rare jewel of a planet.

To claim my full identity in the double dark evolving universe, I have to act consistently with the truths of it. I have to recognize that no God could have been there in the beginning; the miracle is that God is here now. If humanity disappears, God will be extinguished. God is real but no more eternal than we are. I am a process, the universe is a process, and God is a process, too. The biblical God told Moses from the burning bush, "I am becoming what I am becoming," and that statement is inside my truth box. So long as humanity persists, God will keep evolving, becoming whatever it is becoming. I want to conserve this divine explosion of possibilities. The only means of doing so is to preserve our species in all its diversity yet with a comprehension of our unity.

People often ask me, "Do you seriously expect this idea of God to change the world? What about all the fanatics and terrorists?" All I can say is that the only thing that changes the world is an idea that lights our fire at a moment when we are surrounded by dry, dead kindling. Today is that kind of time. Spiritual transformation doesn't require a majority vote. It doesn't matter if most people don't get it. All it takes is a committed minority, because the committed lead culture. The new scientific picture of the universe is a modern revelation. For many the realization that God can be real and is emerging from human aspirations will also be a revelation. That these revelations are both happening now, at so pivotal a moment for our species, is truly grace. They have helped me move into the new universe and feel blessed and awestruck every day, as though I'd moved from a dark basement apartment into a mountain aerie with a hundred-mile view in all directions. I don't expect millions of people to change their ideas of God overnight, but to those who care about the human future and can see beyond ideology, to those who believe that truth matters, and to those who recognize the potential of humanity but don't see how to make us rise to that potential, it could make all the difference to discover a God that is real.

ACKNOWLEDGMENTS

I wish I could explain the gems that each of you has contributed. Thanks and thanks and ever thanks to my brilliant editor, Amy Caldwell, who took a chance on this book, and to Will Myers, Nicholas DiSabatino, and the whole team at Beacon Press; to my agent extraordinaire, Douglas Abrams; my talented artists, Nicolle Rager Fuller and Nina McCurdy; my wise and generous friends Matthew Fox, Deepak Chopra, Rami Shapiro, Candace Calsoyas, Chris Wellens, Billie Hurmence, Leslie Keefe, David Dorfan, and Karen Roekard, who read early drafts and gave me insightful if unsparing feedback; to Ursula Goodenough, whose help with the biological side of emergence was invaluable; and to my meeting, you know who you are. I owe a great and special debt to Archbishop Desmond Tutu and Paul Davies, whose forewords to this book both humble and amaze me. Above all, I am grateful to my husband, Joel Primack; my daughter, Samara Bay; and my mother, Rena Abrams, who are my closest and greatest inspirations, not only in this book but in life.